MW01405450

Dedications

To Frank, for kicking it off so brilliantly.

To Jack, for taking this journey with me.
I can't imagine it without you.
It wouldn't have been. Simple as that.
At least, not half the fun.

To Rio, for your wisdom, your kindness, and your love.
The person that you are. The miracle that you are.

And finally, to David, to the man you've become... always were.
Your integrity and unwavering support.
And, most of all, for allowing this book to happen.
Just as it is.

Preface

I believe we're living a myth. A myth we know nothing about.

And everything that's happening around us, all the craziness in the world, and in our lives, is part of that story. Our story.

What follows, is that myth. Reveals that myth.

I tell this story just as it happened.

Judith Feldman

May 8, 2017

The Myth

Judith Feldman

The Myth

The One we're living that we know nothing about

© 2017 Judith Feldman

All rights reserved.

No part of this document may be reproduced or transmitted in any form or by any means, electronic, mechanical, photocopying, recording, or otherwise, without prior written permission granted by the author.

Requests for permission to make copies of any part of the work should be submitted to the author here:

themythbook@aol.com

Print Version printed in the United States of America
First Printing: July 2017

ISBN-13 number: 978-1548126544

The material in this book cannot substitute for professional advice; further, the author is not liable if the reader relied on the material and was financially damaged in some way, the recollection of stories shared are recalled to the best of the author's knowledge.

The Myth

Table of Contents

Dedications

Preface

Prologue

Part 1 - The Narrative	*1*
Chapter 1 - The Girl	*3*
Chapter 2 - The Girl... Again	*15*
Chapter 3 - And Again...	*25*
Chapter 4 - When the Lion Roared	*35*
Chapter 5 - At Play in the Fields of the Lord	*53*
Chapter 6 - The Wolf	*65*
Part 2 - The Miracle	*81*
Chapter 7 - Hey Jude	*83*
Chapter 8 - By Their Fruits Ye Shall Know Them	*105*
Chapter 9 - For Everything a Season... And a Reason	*107*
Chapter 10 - The Mother of All Puzzle Pieces	*121*
Part 3 - The Myth	*127*
Chapter 11 - In the Beginning	*129*
Chapter 12 - The Mystery Revealed	*137*
Chapter 13 - The Flood	*181*
Chapter 14 - And the Dragon Went to War	*195*
Chapter 15 - The Meaning of Betrayal	*207*
Chapter 16 - The Betrayer	*227*
Chapter 17 - Thirty Minutes of Silence	*241*
Chapter 18 - The Final Chapter	*253*

Epilogue - Infinity and the Mystery of Mind by Antoinette le Roux	259
Appendix I - The Lyrics of Rio Wyles	265
Kick in the Door Remix	267
Malfunction	270
It's Shocking	278
Who Am I?	283
Dancing On the Ceiling	285
Stand Up to Cancer	291
Clear to See	293
We Will Prevail	297
Yonkers Remix	303
No Lie Remix	306
Collision Course	313
Choose Love	317
Appendix II - A Few Short Writings	319
Unemployment As Divine Appointment	321
Dream Big	323
Wall Street, Main Street and God Street	325
Rapunzel, Let Down Your Hair	327
Appendix III Recommended Reading	329

The Myth

Prologue

In 1985, the renowned scholar Joseph Campbell had a conversation with journalist Bill Moyers that resulted in the masterwork, *The Power of Myth*. At the time it first aired, my husband and his Jungian friends were transfixed. But I found the whole thing rather boring. Many years later, as a result of events that had transpired in my own life, a friend suggested I have another look. So I did.

At the end of the first hour, Campbell proposes an interesting theory -- That one can always tell a culture by its tallest building. *"What's informing a society,"* is how he puts it. What the people are about, where they place their focus, their priorities. *"In any medieval town, the tallest building would have been the Cathedral...By the 18th Century, the political palaces."* And in any modern city, he concludes, the tallest structure, by far, *"the office buildings, the centers of economic life."*

Moyers then inquires what Campbell thinks of the race to be the tallest of such buildings in New York. Campbell loved the City, and the magnificence of some of the architecture arising from this competition, but saw hubris in their imagined feelings of superiority, these tallest buildings, scions of industry and finance, of their invincibility amongst the clouds. As he put it so eloquently, *"These Financial Power Centers boldly proclaiming, 'Look what we can do!'"*

Then, Moyers asked the question that left me speechless that day in 2001, as I watched in the aftermath of 9/11:

"Do you think the new myths will come from these buildings?"

Joseph Campbell, *The Power of Myth*

"A myth is a narrative which discloses a sacred world."
--Lawrence J. Hatab, *Myth and Philosophy*

1

The

Narrative

Chapter 1

The Girl

The first time I saw her I was at the gym, on the treadmill, logging in my mandatory forty-five minutes a day. I was new at this, didn't know anyone, and had yet to get my audio gear in gear. So, to stave off boredom I studied the bank across the street, wondering, how it would be robbed? How the security guard would be killed? It's how I made my living.
Writing Crime.
I pictured how it would all go down. Big set piece. Lots of action.
Then out of nowhere, there she was. Dark haired, Hispanic, pretty. About sixteen. On a razor scooter.
It was obvious she'd just gotten the scooter. She wasn't very good at it. But, as she struggled to gain momentum... just to get started... a boy appeared on a skateboard, put his hand on the small of her back, and propelled her forward.

I'd just lost my job. My option on a certain network tv drama wasn't picked up. Not that I was surprised. The experience had been horrific, full of abuse, even for this town. The man running the show was poisonous and determined to destroy every woman in his path. On a show about women.

But the money was great, ridiculously so. So, I kept my head down, knocked out scripts, and collected the checks, along with a daily dose of expletives. Now that was gone. And nothing was appearing in its place.

So, I decided to use the "time off" to take off the weight that had come with the birth of my son. A lot of weight. I had dropped it quickly after he was born, by way of Nutri-System. But over time it had crept back on. I guess my body over the nine months got used to that new plateau, and truth be told, my life over the years had evolved into one of cooking, and working, and escaping into my garden. And I was unhappy enough, although I didn't know it at the time, not to care about any of it.

My marriage had been a struggle from the very first day. Six months in I asked him why he'd married me. All he seemed to do was yell at me. The question was legitimate. I was just asking the wrong person.

"I'm just a big old bear," he'd say, laughing it off. "Ignore it." I tried to, but at some point, I joined in.

And, over the years, more and more, he made my career the center of attention. We were both writers. Not that he didn't like my work. I truly think he was my greatest fan. But, when his own career stalled, and mine was going strong, he simply turned over the reins. I suddenly bore the responsibility of keeping the family afloat.

It wasn't always like that. When I first met him, he had dreams. He'd come to Hollywood years before to add yet another degree to an already pedigree education, this time an M.F.A. from UCLA. His student film drew lots of notice, but it was his documentary work that followed that truly showed his potential as an artist. He was quickly set to do a feature, and his future as a director seemed assured, so assured that he turned down other offers. The advertising industry beckoned, but that held no allure. To hell with the money. He had his eye firmly on the prize. Then his writing career took off with equal energy. He won a noted award for his first script and writing jobs at the Studios quickly followed.

But nothing in this business kills a career faster than a few writing assignments that go nowhere. The studio work dried up and the directing career likewise stalled. By the time I met him, he was making a living writing movies for cable, in a charming cottage on the Venice Canals. And I was an executive at HBO, on my way to becoming a producer. With love in my eyes, I promised him he would direct.

We would make it happen. I would make it happen. And ultimately, he did. I found the money, wrote the script, and he got his shot at directing. He made his movie. But nothing changed. No work came. And now we had a child. A beautiful son named Rio.

So here I was. But I could do this. I could be wife and mother and breadwinner, all in one. Plenty of women perform that juggling act every day. And I was a woman of the sixties and seventies – a feminist. It was almost expected. But more and more that meant I relied on no one, but dreamed of a man who would come and rescue me from all this responsibility. And despite all the evidence to the contrary, I was still hoping that man would be my husband, David.

But, he'd hit a roadblock that he was completely unprepared for. Everything had always come easily. He had no idea how to fight for it. I, on the other hand, was a scrapper. And became the answer. In his mind, and to others, we were just another family struggling to make it in the "business". And I was the lucky one to have work. An Emmy nomination for my first script on *L.A. Law*[1] soon followed, confirming his decision.

Occasionally, we'd fight about it. I wanted him to work, to take on some of the burden. But most of the time, we were too busy making the bills and just relieved when we did. And other times, he'd come through with something just at the right time. And there were moments of happiness. I still loved him and we had Rio. We were a family.

But over time I began to resent the sleeping in and the drinking. And his priding himself on never having worked a day, nine to five. At some point, after years of this, I was done appealing to his ego, the perpetual cheerleader hoping to manipulate him into action. I was finished being understanding. And even though he was still smart as a whip, my respect for him was growing erratic, and the love was fading.

So, I retreated into my garden. And cooking. And endlessly watching Colin Firth in *Pride and Prejudice*, wondering, where's my Darcy? My 'disappearance', no problem for him. Either oblivious or, more likely, relieved. I was leaving him alone. No nagging. No demands.

---

[1] Written along with my writing partner, Sarah Woodside Gallagher

It was only when I lost any desire to make love and stopped making excuses, that we suddenly had a problem. Hadn't we married for richer or poorer? And he still loved me. So, what was my problem?

The truth is with the disintegration of my marriage, that part of me, that sexual part, was deeply asleep. I thought it was over, all of it. That my life was over. I was approaching middle-age. Isn't that what naturally happens? Weren't these final years meant to be lived this way? As an overweight, overwrought woman in her garden, in a marriage full of bickering?

And did I mention that my son was autistic?

How had I drawn this lot?

Up till then, my life had been the stuff of privilege. Easy Street. Postwar America. Philadelphia. Upper middle-class. Educated. Noble even. My grandfather came to this country carrying only a Torah and started the first synagogue in Germantown. And my father was an ethical man in a world where that still mattered. Came back from fighting WWII and went to work for that same grandfather making toys. Their big score, the Davy Crockett hat. Their big miss, a pass on Slinky. "Who's gonna let their kid play on the stairs?" my Aunt challenged over the Seder table.

By the time I came on the scene, my grandfather had retired, and my father was running the place with my lovely Uncle Is. It was a great life. Pretty houses. Golf on Sundays. Parties. Trips to Concord. Margate in the summer. A real 50's dream. Tragedy was not part of the picture. My greatest disappointment to this point was not getting into Penn. Sure, there were minor heartbreaks, and I didn't win that

Emmy, but nothing, not even the disappointment and disintegration of my marriage and relationship with David, could hold a candle to the tragedy of Rio.

My son from the day he was born was charming and smart, and extraordinary looking. At two-and-a-half, interested in opera, figure skating, and already hitting balls on a tennis court. He was a neat guy and attracted people like a magnet. They said he looked like an angel. And he did.

And appeared to be developing normally. Any deficiency escaped my first-time mother eyes or for that matter the teachers at his lovely private pre-school, as well as a first-rate pediatrician. To their credit, this was the first wave of autism to hit this country. No one was looking for it back in '91. But little signs began to appear. He'd spin when he'd watch the skating, but then again, so were they.

But when the other boys in school began to show an interest in more intricate toys, I watched as Rio stared longingly at the playground equipment out the window. But they assured me he was developing -- just a little slower. Not unusual for a boy. And his language was good. And his gross motor was right on target.

But then one day he stopped talking. His words suddenly disappeared. Vanished. Just like that. Almost all that is. He'd look at me and ask "What's your name?" over and over. His gait grew clumsy and his eyes began to cloud over. I was losing him.

"*I know you want me to tell you there's nothing wrong with your son,*" the neurologist got right to the point. "But there is. He's autistic."

She had him walk on a line like some drunk.

"*You might want to contact the Regional Center. Eventually, he'll require assisted living -- A social worker to check in on him, assuming he's up to living on his own, or a group home. The state will financially assist you. I don't have the number. They're listed.*"

And she was gone.

I was too stunned to cry. She had begun saying all of this in front of Rio, but I asked that the nurse take him out front to play. I didn't want him to hear. Now four, the doctor just assumed he wouldn't understand, but I was sure he could.

I refused to accept the news. The speech therapist we'd already engaged was optimistic of his language returning, and he was responding. I held back the tears for days. I didn't want him to see me cry. In fact, I didn't cry until that weekend in Barnes & Noble, searching for evidence I knew was there that would negate her finding; wipe away the diagnosis. For the prognosis that was laid out in every book on autism was more than I could handle. It was a death sentence.

And as I ran out of the bookstore, I broke down. This wasn't my son they were talking about. But it was. More and more. And as horrible as it sounds, and as much as I love him, every inch of him, I cried for my life, as well as his. It was my death sentence as well. To hell with their: *"You planned for Paris but you ended up in Amsterdam,"* I wanted Paris. *Somebody get me to Paris!*

So, like most people in a country and a generation where everything seemed possible, we went into action. David was a champ, suddenly strong. He got me out of my funk, and onto a plan. We'd get him the best help, the best doctors... early intervention. We'd beat this.

And any disappointment, any pain, and there was plenty of it -- as I watched Rio struggle with the simplest task, his little body shaking on overload -- as my friends' children developed normally and increasingly shunned him -- *that pain,* was buried beneath the roses in my garden, and, in the dishes I prepared from all parts of the Mediterranean. And the pounds came back on.

An illness like this can either pull a family together or tear them apart. In our case, it was a little of both. Rio became our life's work. But if I ever were to think of leaving, that was now an impossibility. I needed David in order to get through this. I couldn't do it on my own.

And over time, as Rio's language returned, but in an odd, ritualistic, repetitive manner, as well as his behavior, I let go of any dream of a normal life for him, of soccer games, swimming, camp, dances, girls, first love, first kiss, friends, let alone college and marriage. Or ever living on his own. The neurologist was right. We'd need the Regional Center and any other help we could get. For now, there were Doctors' bills, and Speech bills, and O.T. bills, and vision therapy bills, and sensory integration bills.

A week at U.C.L.A. alone clocked in at a cool twenty-five grand. All of this early intervention was costing us in the neighborhood of seventy-five thousand a year, and the insurance company was fighting us on every dime. We were going broke fast. And David's drinking quickly went beyond social, or fun. The weight was the least of my problems.

But, as any woman who is overweight will tell you, let alone middle-aged, to the world she is invisible. I still saw myself as attractive, but no one else did, maybe other than David. But when I looked at pictures, I was horrified.

So, when I lost my job with the abusive boss, knowing that Rio was getting the best of everything, every doctor, every school, every tutor, I told him it was his turn to support the family. I needed a break. I needed to be relieved of all this pressure. I was met with a blank stare and silence. And a lecture on the essential role he was playing. He was, after all, the one who got him all those tutors, found those teachers and doctors, fought the insurance, got him those services. What do you think you'd pay a lawyer?

He was right. Absolutely.

But you're his father.

We were both being selfish. Immature.

Retreating to our corners. Girding for the next round.

Wherever it was coming from.

The ad I'd clipped from the paper promised quick weight loss. The "before" pictures showed women much like me, middle-aged and overweight. The "after" photos were all very "va- va- va- voom". Not exactly what I had in mind.

I just wanted myself back.

So, I went in that first day determined to do just that.

And met Frank.

And the girl on the scooter.

Chapter 2
The girl... Again

The next time I saw her was three weeks later and ten pounds lighter. By now the treadmill and I were great friends. There she was again, exactly as before, across the street, in front of the bank, on the scooter.
Only this time she was gettin' good at it, doing lazy figure eights.
But there was that boy again. Came right up behind her, put his hand on the small of her back, and propelled her forward.

Frank had come highly recommended. In fact, the people from the ad insisted there was no better trainer for me. He was smart, interesting, and a genius at knocking weight off women. Somehow, they neglected to mention gorgeous. And mesmerizing. Or maybe, that's what made him so successful.

It took about a day for us to become great friends. After dropping Rio at school, we'd spend hours talking on the bikes or the treadmill. Finding the right school for Rio had been no easy task. By third grade he'd been to eleven, sometimes driving clear across town on the reputation of a teacher, or a pilot program. Someone, who might understand him. Somewhere, where he might make progress.

And he did. But nowhere near what we'd expected, given all the intervention. At nine, he still couldn't hold a pencil. He couldn't even find it, even if it was sitting on the desk right in front of him. He was barely reading and had every learning disability known to man in addition to ADD, OCD and a touch of Tourette's. And stringing together a comprehensible sentence was a dream unrealized. His speech was strange and ritualized. Nonsensical. And endlessly repetitive.

Every year he dropped further and further behind his peers, despite all his hard work and the extraordinary effort of the professionals who were treating him. His daily life was an unending struggle. Watching him brought tears to my eyes and broke my heart, and earned him my respect. All in a single moment.

So, I was only too happy in my free time to escape all that at the gym with Frank, where we'd share our favorite books, art, movies, music. And he'd tell me stories of his childhood in northern Germany. Some very funny, most terribly sad. If you've ever wondered what it was like growing up in the wake of Hitler, and the effect the Nazi movement had on its people, Frank's life spoke volumes, although the worst of it only alluded to.

Born to a father who abandoned the family months before his birth, and a mother who placed him in a series of foster homes, many of which were abusive, then ultimately an orphanage, where he fled to a forest to hide every day. Occasionally she'd bring him home, with promises as she unpacked his suitcase, that she'd never leave him again, only to return him the next morning, after a night of wild drinking, and partying, and men. And the view from his bedroom window on these visits? A working sixteenth-century farm. In reality, an ongoing installation at the local museum next door. But to a boy living in fear and horror, it was magic. Perfection. By eighteen, he contemplated a life on the dole or becoming a hitman. All in all, a story worthy of Gunter Grass.

But all that seemed behind him. He was in great spirits now. He glowed. Right from the start, his conversation was peppered with references to the Universe and concepts of spirituality. Buddhist tales. New thought. Ancient Wisdom.

Half the time I didn't know what he was talking about, but I didn't care. I was happy. I was having fun. And I'd never heard any of this before and was thoroughly enjoying myself. And for the first time in years, I thought maybe my life wasn't over. Maybe I was being given another chance. And with all this working out -- and he was a great trainer -- the years spent in unhappiness seemed to be disappearing from my face, along with the weight.

"A beautiful woman with luminous eyes and a luminous smile," was how he described me one day, "whose light had almost gone out."

But no more.

I remember so clearly standing in my garden that first month thinking, it feels like it's Christmas in July. That wonderful feeling you have at Christmas, but in the middle of summer.

Sometime in September, I gave Frank a CD to thank him for all his kindness and support, with a note on a glittery miniature Christmas card, the only one on hand that morning. And after that, whenever I'd walk into the gym, no matter where he was, or who he was with, or the temperature outside here in sunny California, he'd begin to whistle a Christmas tune. People would look at him strangely and wonder aloud:

"Christmas, Frank? Little early."

I was charmed.

Eventually, our time at the gym extended to lunch, then tea, and hikes, or hours at the bookstore. No question I was neglecting my family. But the home front was a heartache; an abyss. I needed a break. I needed some happiness before going back in. Like the mother on the plane that's out of oxygen. And given the quality of Frank's character and attention, I was falling in love.

Then one Sunday he called to check our time for training the next morning. He'd never called the house before, and there was no reason to that day. But Sunday was the only day we didn't see each other. With David in the next room, like lovers we talked briefly and cryptically. I knew he'd been out on his motorcycle in the mountains, somewhere in Topanga. I asked him how the ride was. He told me he'd been thinking of me. How much I'd love it there.

There, it was. Out. He was thinking of me. As I was thinking of him.

"Maybe we could go sometime," I managed.

"How 'bout next week?" he asked, not a trace of hesitation.

As much as I wanted to say yes, I knew it was impossible. I couldn't get on the back of that motorcycle without telling David. And how could I tell him? What could I tell him? Knowing it was exactly what it looked like. And I wasn't about to lie. Not on that level. I heard David leave the room.

"I'll have to ask David."

"Of course, I assumed you would." His voice took cover.

The next morning Frank was waiting outside when I arrived.

"Well, are we going? Did you ask? Are we on?"

I told him I thought it was dangerous.

"No more dangerous than crossing the street."

I couldn't tell if he was being coy or simply naïve. I studied his face. This wasn't like him.

"I'm not talking about the bike," I added. "I've been on a motorcycle."

Then, to my surprise, he looked at me incredulously. It appeared I was the one that was naïve. Or delusional. There was nothing going on between us. He made that perfectly clear. And if there was, it was all in my mind. There was nothing to hide from David, or anyone. We were friends. Just friends.

I was stunned.

Obviously, I'd been out of the game for some time and rusty. And there'd been nothing physical. But the sexual tension was thick. And in the past, anyone who had spent the amount of time, and the kind of time Frank and I had spent together, definitely wanted something. And it was usually love. Silly me.

"Sorry," I managed. "Wrong guy," and walked away.

But it was too late to completely walk away. There was too much feeling there, and we both wanted to put this glitch behind us as quickly as possible. Pretend it never happened. Go back to the way things had been. With the unspoken understanding that it would never happen again.

But it did. One day, he looked at me with such love, but later swore in a note that he would conquer this. Conquer what? These feelings? Why would he want to?

I began to see a shrink as soon as this whole thing started. Believe it or not, I was taking all of it, my marriage, David, Frank, very seriously. She told me she didn't want me leaving David unless I was totally sure right down to my toes. And helped me understand that given Frank's upbringing, intimacy may be a real problem. That there was a strong likelihood we'd never be more than loving friends.

Still, even knowing all this about him, I blew at his declaration. I told him if he was hell bent on conquering this, if he truly wasn't interested, to leave me alone, to knock off the conversations, the hours spent together, the intimate conversations, the seduction, all of it. Once again, he denied any feelings for me. Only this time his denial was full of rage.

We ultimately seemed to make peace. But when I went in to train two days later, he kept his distance and, at the end of the session, which I thought went pretty well considering, he told me he wanted me to leave the gym. For a week... To go to the beach and walk as close to the water as possible. From the Venice pier to the jetty, and back. No company, no music, no exercise. Just walk. Get rid of this energy. Give it up. To the ocean.

"Are you banishing me?"

It was for my own good, he assured me. But I wondered as I left, whose good was it for? And what energy I was to get rid of? Love? I was crushed. And livid. What a coward he was. And wondered what kind of deranged trip I'd wandered into.

Still, the next day I headed to the beach, as instructed. Angry as I was, I couldn't just stay home and had nowhere else to go. And I was the good girl following orders.

But, as I stepped onto the beach, my rage at Frank began to bubble up and pour out of me. "Fuck you, Frank. Fuck you!" I could hear myself, tears coming, anger surging. Desperation grew with each step forward. This wasn't going to work. The remedy and the perpetrator were all too entwined. There was no ridding myself of this energy – his energy -- not this way. Not here. Not in this place where he sent me. And that's all I wanted to do was rid myself of him. Forget him. To stop hurting. Most of all to stop hurting!!!

But when I took a few more steps forward and looked out at the ocean, the strangest thing happened. I started to laugh. Uncontrollably. Barrels of it. From out of nowhere. And I was filled with the most wonderful feeling I had ever experienced in my life. Joy. Pure Joy. Unadulterated Joy.

Nothing, not my happiest moments, my greatest achievements, not even the birth of my son, had come close to this. This was different. The quality of the feeling. It was like I'd been sprinkled with fairy dust. A ton of it. And at that moment, the whole world changed, literally, physically. The colors, rich and saturated. It was beautiful, like a painting. And I was filled with Love.

And as I proceeded down the beach from the pier to the jetty, as instructed, with this beatific look on my face, small iridescent birds circled around me. I had no idea what was happening. I'd certainly been to the beach before. I only lived a block away.

But for the next seven days, I went to the beach. And for seven days I took one look at the ocean and started to laugh. Three days in I realized it wasn't me laughing. That something was experiencing its creation through me. The magnificence of it. All the while telling me, *This is the way you're supposed to feel all the time.* Joy. Who knew?

"Joy," I heard preached shortly after that, having found my way to the local spiritual center, Agape, "is evidence that God is on the playing field."

God??? Are you kidding me? Playing field? This thing called "God" is real??? Not just some concept or belief system?

But there was no denying it. I was having an experience of God every day on that beach. Of Love and Light pouring through me. As tangible as the coffee I was drinking. Right there, just south of the Venice Pier.

"Don't fly away," my mother warned me, amused.

Midweek I wrote Frank and told him he was in danger of losing me. That I may never come back... from this paradise. This feeling.

But Monday morning I did. I couldn't stay away. I missed my friends and all the fun. And I missed him. But I came back a very different person. Everyone gathered around to welcome me. I was tan and glowing. And across the room, Frank finished with a client and ran to me, joking, as he pushed through the small crowd.

"Move aside," he ordered. "Let me see her." Then took one look at my eyes, as if he knew all along what was about to happen.

That he was my angel.

His mission accomplished.

The story had begun.

Chapter 3

And Again...

*Shortly after that, I saw her again. The girl.
I had a dream about leaving David.
I hadn't actually said those words before.
It was a terrible dream. David and I were separating and
arguing over who would take care of Rio.
And neither one of us wanted to.*

I woke up crying, ashamed. As much as I loved Rio, every delicious part of him, the very thought of going it alone terrified me, and I was sure David in his anger would bail on me, Rio, and any sense of responsibility as soon as I left. He'd already threatened as much. It would be mine to handle, alone. All of it.

So, as I left the house that Sunday morning and headed for the gym, by the time I reached the front door, I'd made up my mind. I didn't want that to happen. To take on this child completely on my own. I couldn't. Even if David had made no effort to find work, he was tireless in his fight for

Rio, making sure he got everything he needed. The thought of doing it all was too overwhelming. One ball too many in that juggling act. So, as I turned the key in the door locking it behind me, I swore off the idea of leaving. Of divorcing David. Of breaking up this family. No, I didn't want that.

But, as I turned around, through the canapé of trees in front of my house, through the rose covered arbor, there she was... the girl on the scooter. And, as she glided by, the boy appeared right behind her, put his hand on the small of her back, and propelled her forward.

"But I do want that!" I heard myself exclaim. The words hung in the air.

I do want that. That love. That support. And I still assumed it would come from a man. But, it was pretty clear that it wasn't going to be David, regardless of my decision to stay. Or Frank, for that matter. Oh, we'd have our moments, great times, when I'd leave him covered in his energy, desiring him. But any attempt at a date was disastrous, replete with his inability to breathe and breaking out in a rash. Then he met another woman, and even though she quickly betrayed him, I shut down. It was over. And the attraction was gone as abruptly as it had arrived.

But what I was left with most of all, was my time at the beach, which had become the most important time of my day. I began to meditate. I was still big on the walk, from the pier to the jetty, but at some point, I knew instinctively to sit and close my eyes and open my heart. I wanted to hold onto the wonderful feeling I walked into that day, and sure enough, within moments, I was filled with love. Waves of it. And light. And peace.

I also wanted to understand it and read anything I could get my hands on – from Marianne Williamson to Iyanla Vanzant, Deepak Chopra, Gary Zukov, Neale Walsh, and scores of others – and to tell anyone and everyone I could, what had happened. That this thing called God is real!

Because, despite dismal circumstances at home, no job in sight for either one of us, and the continuing tragedy of Rio, despite it all, I was filled with an indescribable, unexplainable joy. No matter what happened in any given 24-hour period, I had the beach and this feeling, guaranteed. Every morning... without fail.

But, why? Why was this happening to me? The question nagged. I wasn't seeking a spiritual life, or, for that matter, a relationship with God. I wasn't even aware there was one to be had. I'd always believed in a God, pretty much based on nothing. Occasionally prayed to one. But organized religion had left me cold. And bored. Responsive reading, standing up, sitting down. It delivered nothing for me other than a guilt-laden obligation to occasionally attend out of a fear of a God who judged you if you missed. Particularly on the High Holidays. By college, I'd stopped worrying and stopped going.

But this was different. Not some blind belief or wishful thinking. Or guilt-driven anything. This was real. Tangible. There was no denying this. It was too big.

The truth is, the awakening on the beach wasn't my first brush with this feeling. I recognized it from when I was a teenager at the Jersey Shore. I'd go to the beach with my friends and we'd douse ourselves with Coppertone, and with reflectors in hand we'd toast, emerging tanned and beautiful. And having a great time doing it. But sometimes, when I'd close my eyes under that sun, I'd feel that light moving through me. I didn't know what it was back then, and frankly, it scared the heck out of me. I'd quickly open my eyes. Eventually, it stopped trying.

And over the years there'd been the odd coincidence, the prescient dream, but compared to this moment, the magnitude of the experience, on this level, there'd only been one prior occurrence that came remotely close. The morning after my marriage to David.

We had just made love. It was pleasurable, but no different than any other time, despite the significance. But it began with a wedding that wasn't particularly loving, or romantic, or fun, at least not for me. Not one surprise. Not one kiss caught off-guard. Call me a hopeless romantic. I am. But David was enjoying entertaining on that scale, and it seems a good time was had by all that New Year's Eve, so I was happy. I busied myself being the hostess. But feeling lonely. Pleased, but not in love, at least not the way I should have been. Not the way I know now I can be. No one sweeping me off my feet. So, I put off making love till the following morning.

And it was nice. It always was. But this time, that morning after, when it was over, as we lay connected, a feeling came over us. We looked at each other. What the heck was going on? It was like a golden blanket was being lowered on us and we were being blessed. A stamp of approval from the great beyond. Right there, in a bungalow at The Hotel Bel Air.

The rest of that weekend was business as usual. Once again, not a speck of romance, or real love. Not what I had imagined a honeymoon would be. The courtship was over. And whatever we had experienced in that curious moment was never brought up. Somehow it got lost.

But not forgotten. At least not by me. And when I would bring it up over time, David would agree that it occurred and felt honored for having been singled out that way. But had absolutely no interest in exploring it. He was in charge of his life, subject to no greater authority. Master of his fate. Simple as that.

But it came into my thoughts from time to time, initially keeping me there in that marriage. A union that had been blessed regardless of its failings. But why would God...any God.... bless a relationship that was ultimately miserable? Could it be, I thought, that we were meant to produce a child? This child? Who could barely utter a sentence? Lost in the complexity of the simplest task, wondering where to begin? Ever more isolated. Unable to keep up. Internally, I was crying all the time.

And there'd been a dream.

2049 Century Park East

It was in '95, shortly after Rio's diagnosis. I had just come back from Russia, where Sarah and I were writing a mini-series for British TV on a serial killer. My agent told me we didn't stand a chance of getting back into the series game, increasingly flooded with writers edged out of features. The medical bills were mounting and the movies of the week we were engaged to write weren't paying nearly enough.

So purely out of necessity, I flirted with the idea of returning to law. It'd been 15 years since I'd left the bar and a practice in entertainment law, and no one was exactly waiting for my return. It wasn't gonna be easy, but I had faith in my ability to pull it off. But the idea of abandoning my career as a writer, to help others realize theirs, was just too depressing. No, if I went back, this time I'd represent kids like Rio. Fight the good fight against insurance giants and schools who increasingly wanted no part of these kids. Yes, I'd become a professional pain in the ass for good causes. Kind of like my own ACLU. Maybe move to Washington. Hmmm...this is starting to sound pretty good.

But the thought of going back to law in any fashion completely bummed me out. And, I wasn't through being a writer. Hollywood is a lot like Vegas. It's hard to step away from the table when you're convinced that next job is the big score that will catapult you to where you belong, at the very top, with the elite, recognized for your talent, your vision. At which point I'd get to make all the movies I had come to this town to make. And the work we'd just done in Russia was by far our best. The Brits who'd hired us were delighted. And there was a buzz around town about our script. Leaving was going to be anything but easy.

At which point I had the dream.

In the dream, I was at a party on the 41st floor of 2049 Century Park East in Century City, part of an enclave of swank office buildings, a stone's throw from BH. I'd actually had an office there at one time, as an executive for HBO ten years before, and had attended lots of parties just like the one in my dream, part of the American Film Market. Only this was no A-list party or even B – no this was strictly "C" list, I remember being told. No stars here, no big names. Just hustlers, and earnest businessmen from all over the world. Men in turbans, buyers from Indonesia, that sort of thing. Suddenly, in the midst of this, a man came in, wielding a gun, and threatened to kill everyone in the room, unless someone could introduce him to Shania Twain.

"Shania Twain?!

What the heck is some country star doing in my dream?" I remember thinking.

And, regrettably, as so often the case in Hollywood, no one in the room knew Shania, nor could anyone get to her. We were all doomed. But he let three people survive -- a guy who had been nice to him when he came in the room, a child, and me, for I was to accompany the child to the entertainment center on the second floor.

The kid leaves, I follow, much relieved not to be dying, and find myself entering a kind of Chuckee Cheese, all bells and whistles. The kid runs for the skeeball, and, as I step towards the center, the building suddenly begins to implode from the top. The guy's set a bomb off and we're all gonna die.

"Why did you stay in the building??!!!" "He let you go." "Why did you come here?" These thoughts race through my mind and

flood my consciousness as I run for the door, remember the child, and look back.

And woke up. David was asleep next to me, completely unaware that my entire body was shaking, uncontrollably. The image of the building falling on me was so real. I knew immediately what the dream was saying: Get out of the building --- The entertainment center --The business.

But it was only a dream. I mean do you really make life choices based on a dream? But I remembered every detail. I'd never had a dream like this. But even so, law sucked.

"You've got to help me with this transition," I heard myself saying, knowing how difficult, make that impossible, walking away would be. But why I prayed at that moment, still remains a mystery. I'd never appealed to God in that way, as if tangible help was available. But some part of me was taking this dream very seriously, and knew I needed all the help I could get. The will I knew I lacked. But as soon as I got the words out, as if in conversation, I heard a voice move through me, as clear as day:

"*I gave you the child.*"

Even the way he said it, especially the way he said it, I knew it wasn't me talking.

Well, I thought, I'd gotten the child in the dream and he almost saved me. And I had Rio. Maybe I really was meant to help these kids. Fight the good fight. Go back to Law.

But I wasn't ready. I'm ashamed to say I took no steps in that direction, and a month or so later, with the most minute effort, landed a big job with a new series. I was back in the game. With the abusive boss who screamed at me daily.

Now that was gone.

And Frank was gone.

I find it amusing that when God chose to speak to me, it came in the form of a romance, all tangled up. I think this God knew that if he got too serious on me too quickly, I would have blown him off. It would have turned me off. But in the form of a great looking German trainer, it was irresistible.

Then the real story began to unfold. A myth full of passion and betrayal and love. It would take a far better player than Frank to pull that off. God had something in mind, and he had the perfect guy to do it.

And the dream? It was never far from my thoughts. It shared a space with the golden blanket from my honeymoon.

And from time to time I wondered about Rio being that child I was given.

And what the hell Shania Twain was doing in my dream...?

Chapter 4

When The Lion Roared

Someone called me an angel the other day.

I don't know about this angel stuff, but could there really be something called God?? I'd had an experience of God, right here... on this very beach, at this very spot, just months before. I closed my eyes, remembering that day, and when I opened them, there was a bottle of champagne at my feet, the cork perched precariously on top.

"Was that bottle here when I closed my eyes?" I wondered.

Suddenly, I began to cry.

I came to this town to make movies. Great movies. Like Selznick and Thalberg. I had big dreams, and a first-rate creative mind in my writing partner, Sarah.

Our first pitch was with the president of MGM, back when the lion still roared over there in Culver City. It was a vibrant studio back then, and as I walked onto the lot that day, I could feel the ghosts of Mickey Rooney and Judy Garland. It was palpable. And there we were, our first time up, in the office of the president -- luxe, deco, with vases of Casablanca lilies. The stuff dreams are made of.

It was a great pitch, wowed the audience, the centerpiece of which was a bottle of champagne, the use of which had ingeniously and spontaneously occurred to me.

It recalled a scene from Hitchcock's *Notorious*. In that movie, Cary Grant plays a handler, a spy in Buenos Aires, assigned to recruit and manage a beautiful girl with a past and a questionable allegiance, played magnificently by Ingrid Bergman. In this scene, he gets an unexpected call to meet with his superiors. He agrees, and stops by on the way to her place. What they don't know -- and he's just discovering himself-- is that he's fallen in love with her, despite himself. To add to the danger of the affair he's about to embark on, he arrives at the meeting flaunting a bottle of champagne, that he now brazenly places on the table. For the first time, he hears the details of her dangerous assignment and another nugget of her questionable past. Hitchcock cleverly plays the entire scene on the bottle, and the unasked questions that hang in the air. "Who's the champagne for? Where's he headed? What does this all mean?"

Like their story, the Champagne in our pitch represented the concept that "Nothing is as it appears to be". Not in their story. Not in ours. And, I'm beginning to see, as this memory from so long ago suddenly dropped by with a message, not in the one I'm living right now.

And, as I looked down at the bottle on the beach, tears came to my eyes. For I had just asked the question, "Could there really be something called God?" And when I opened them, I heard a voice, gently chiding:

*"**Who do you think thought of the champagne?**"*

I laughed and marveled at the thought of a God with a sly sense of humor. I picked up the bottle and walked to the jetty, where I was meeting someone. I couldn't wait to tell him.

"Left over from the prom?" he asked with a nod to the bottle.
"Got time for a story?" I responded.

I already knew the answer. It was seven o'clock on a Sunday morning. Neither one of us was goin' anywhere.

I'd met him on the beach, in passing, literally. I was walking in one direction. He was jogging in the other. We obviously were on similar schedules, had been presumably for months before I laid eyes on him one day, when I looked up to find his, on me. Granted, it was the tail end of Frank, but still, how could I have missed him? This was not a guy you miss. More like a vision, graced with the natural gait of an athlete, and patrician good looks.

The following day I watched as he came into view, the perfect run, the graceful toss of the Frisbee into the ocean to his Golden, the dog leaping through the waves to retrieve it, all done without missing a beat. Set against a rising sun and a pink and blue winter sky.

Within days we added a *Hi* and *Morning* to our exchange. Then I saw Frank at Agape with his new romance. He proudly introduced her. Took me by surprise like a well-placed punch to the stomach. And all my joy went south. The next morning I was in no mood for hellos from strangers, so when he jogged by, I mumbled something and quickly looked away.

The next day, thank God, I was back to feeling more like me, and offered a bright and shiny "Morning!", as he strode by. His response was cold, all the prior enthusiasm gone. "I feel better!" I called after him, wanting to explain. "Good," he added curtly. I watched him disappear. It felt oddly like a fight. And we hadn't even met.

I forgot him after that. Life called and I shifted my schedule, and got lost again in the beauty of the beach. And the feeling that I was walking with God.

Then one morning, I arrived late. By the time I hit the beach, the sun was out full blast. I started my walk from the pier to the jetty then stopped at some point to remove my sweater, and felt someone's eyes on me. I looked over at the parking lot a distance away. There he was, at an impromptu gathering of dogs and their owners, the others oblivious, as he watched me unbutton every button. Never taking his eyes off me. And I obliged. A simple task suddenly charged.

We met the next day.

This time I was a little smarter. But not by much. The signs were obscured, and the package was heady bait. He was a first-rate writer, successful, great looking and smart. And athletic. And all man. Even a married male friend of mine called him a hunk.

And, if that wasn't enough, he'd walked away from it all, much like me, to pursue something greater: A dream to paint. And just for good measure, he owned a house on the beach, another in the mountains, when he needed to get away, and a family ranch of about 4500 head of cattle, and God knows how many acres. He'd ride off into the sunset every few months. A cowboy and a poet, who looked like William Hurt or Harrison Ford, I could never decide.

To a woman who came of age in the late 60's early 70's, there are certain actors that are downright fatal. Harrison Ford was in *Working Girl*. Sometimes Jack Nicolson was. And always William Hurt. The guy was the perfect embodiment of intelligence and athleticism and picked his roles wisely enough to include humility. Someone who made mistakes and admits it. You believed him. No woman can resist that. Which is what makes guys like Hurt so dangerous. My new friend was just that kind of guy. And divorced.

"How is it flying free?" I asked one morning as we parted, as I toyed with my own marital future.

"My favorite state!" he called back, all smiles.

On that note, my mother would have had all the warning flags up flapping. *Stop signs*, she calls them. Sorry, mom.

"My ex-wife's a great girl," he added. "But our sex life was a disaster."

Pretty intimate stuff for eight a.m. at the beach, casually tossed off. But my best friend finished his thought, "But with you, it'll be different." It still felt too soon.

But what followed were great mornings full of laughter, and sharing our lives, our childhood, in a way I had never done with anyone before. It was like the best date you ever had. Every day.

"Have you been to the other side?" he asked one morning a few weeks in, his face belying nothing.

I smiled at the layers contained in that question, and what followed was pure magic.

I spent that morning perched on a rock on the "other side" of the jetty, he the perfect distance below, tossing the Frisbee to his dog, who'd leap into the channel, then scurry back up the rocks. He regaled me with stories of summers at a house on the lake, small-town parades, a day lost in his life when he was seven, his mother finding him wandering dazed on a back-country road. He was convinced he'd been abducted by a UFO. A shotgun third marriage in Vegas, that lasted less than a week. I imagined some ditzy blonde a la Monroe, with thick glasses, blind as a bat, running around in his shirt, right out of *Gentlemen Prefer Blondes*. I laughed. He marveled at me. That I wasn't judging him. It's easy when you don't know all the facts. He told me of a career in Europe playing baseball. Didn't mention the brief one here in football. I only found that out later from a third party. "Why bother?" would have been his attitude. "Never made it out of training camp." For most of us, making it to a pro training camp would have been something to crow about. But not him. He was private and understated. The perfect hero.

Then, a mist came in enveloping us.

He held onto me when we finally said goodbye. "That was beautiful," he said. "Really beautiful."

And it was.

I was dead meat.

To make matters worse, his friend owned a café on the beach and one day offered to open it just for us, in the early hours, as we stood outside talking in the rain, not wanting to part. After that, it became a daily ritual - meet up by the water, then head to the café, where he'd wash down the wonderful Max, rinse my feet, and we'd talk for hours, drinking coffee spiked with whatever he'd grab from behind the bar. The place was ours. All ours. And he'd read aloud to me from the paper.

"Tell me what's going on in the story?" I'd ask. And he'd report on the news from around the world, whatever he thought I should know. Then onto obscure facts... *this day in history*... that sort of thing. And always ending with my horoscope. Then I'd make him read his. And more and more something swirled in the air around us. Binding us. Enchanting us. It was getting harder and harder to pull away.

But it never went beyond those mornings, even as they got longer and longer, sometimes extending well into the afternoon. And never away from that spot. Once again, I was dealing with a man who was afraid of intimacy. I knew the signs. His failed marriages. A mother who was less than kind. And he, from time to time, remote. Distant. We talked about it. Was he interested? What did it mean? I needed to know while I could still get out, even though I knew it was already too late. He copped to being moody. But, also confessed there was another woman. In Cuba. He'd met her a year before and had recently visited. I remembered the trip. He'd gone to a wedding in Mexico then hopped a plane to Havana. He'd told me all about it. Hemingway's room, the magic of the old city. Somehow, he forgot to mention her.

He'd gotten very sick after he returned and disappeared. "Jungle fever," he said when he finally surfaced.

Now he was coming clean. Sort of. "You're my last best chance for a relationship," he said. The whole time he spoke, Max stood by my side, actually between my legs. He knew something was wrong. That I might leave. But I didn't. I couldn't. He made me feel beautiful whenever I was with him and even when I wasn't.

"You are beautiful," he wrote. "Maybe I'm just a good mirror."

Isn't that what a woman wants to feel? Desired and beautiful? I felt like the girl in high school who gets the quarterback. The most popular guy. The guy all the other girls are in love with. And they were. But it was more than that. He was the quarterback and the most popular guy because of the quality of the human being. An innate quality. I think I fell in love with him early one morning when he was standing by the water's edge, with a group of people, hanging out, talking, throwing the Frisbee to Max, when a wave suddenly broke, dangerously high, catching all of them unaware. I watched from the pier, as everyone fled. Everyone but him, as he lifted a small child high into the air, above the water that would have taken her, forgotten by her own father in his own panic. A hero. A genuine hero. And an intelligence, and wit, and heart that easily earned him the title.

And an energy so thick that it began to weave a thread between us, that reminded me of the line from *Jane Eyre*, as delivered by Welles... "Oh, Jane, Jane, I feel like there's a string attached to my heart, that's attached to yours."

I'd never felt this way before.

"I had a dream about you last night," he offered a month or so after we'd met. "I was sitting at a table, writing, on simple brown parchment. It was my writing, but it was your spirit that was infusing my words. And the writing was silver and gold."

I was flattered. Who wouldn't be?

He told me magic was beginning to happen in his life, strange coincidences, and was convinced it was all me. "I think you've pierced the veil. Seen the other side. And you're taking me with you."

"No, it's your life... whatever magic, is your doing....you're bringing it in.... including me." Trying out these new age concepts, struggling to really understand manifestation and reality through thought, and loving the fact he disagreed. "No, it's you."

"I'm with him." My shrink weighed in. "You're connecting him to the Universe. You're his angel. Like Frank was to you."

He liked that, his angel, and in his emails, I was suddenly a.j. "Is that me?" I wrote. "Yes," he responded, "Angel Judy". I loved it. That he'd given me a nickname and that it was so waspy. Where I grew up, and when I grew up, Anglo-Saxon was the thing. Everyone wanted to be blond and Protestant and dressed in Villager. So, a.j. was just swell.

And he signed the letter, j.a... a.j. and j.a... aj and ja.

Opposites? Reflection? Other half?

Certainly felt that way. Like we were a reflection, opposites, all of it. Bone of my bone. Once again, I'd never felt this way before.

"I wish I could go with you," I said one morning as we headed off the beach, he onto the mountains. "So do I," he responded, without a moment's hesitation. We were falling in love. At least I was. And I think he was.

Then God showed up again. This time for the two of us.

I thrust the champagne bottle into the sand, and proceeded to tell him the story, just like I told you. The lion roaring... the ghosts of MGM... the champagne, the pitch. And God's sly retort.

"Am I crazy to be talking in terms of God?" I asked him.

"Look where you put the champagne," was all he said.

I looked down, and there it was, in the middle of a heart someone had drawn that morning, about three feet across on that huge expanse of a beach, in which they'd written the word: 'God'.

The bottle was over the 'G' and the 'O'.[2]

He threw the Frisbee to Max in the water, and when we turned back, the bottle was gone.

We saw each other every morning. And every day was like a party. Max kicking it off with a howl, throwing his head back, letting loose, as soon as he saw me approach. Even before that, I'd watch as he picked up my scent.

---

[2] Only years later would someone point out another possible message in that bottle. In the placement of it. Can you see it?

"Where's Judy?" Jack would tease, over and over. Max would bark and howl, racing between us, closing the distance.

"Yes, Judy's here." It certainly felt like love. It was beautiful.

I was convinced more than ever that my life wasn't over. There was more to be had. Perhaps a chance at real love. That God was real and amongst us, and better than any jdate or match.com. And once again, it allowed me to face the overwhelming sadness of Rio. The tragedy of Rio. No cure. No real progress. Just the grim reality of Autism settling in. Thanks to Jack, I was able to approach my new normal with love and happiness in my heart.

But good as it was, he was always leaving. To the mountains. To the Ranch. He was looking for a new home. A new life. He made that perfectly clear. He was itchin' for an adventure and this wasn't it. I wasn't it. But if I'd miss a day to avoid getting in any deeper, to protect myself, there'd be an edge when I returned, a subtle anger, a hurt. Then he'd remind me he's leaving. I couldn't win. My shrink offered that he was angry because he was feeling something that could potentially foil his plans. That I might keep him here.

Like George in *It's a Wonderful Life* in that extraordinary scene when he takes Donna Reed by the shoulders, shaking her. *"I don't want any plastics and I don't want any ground floors,"* he orders, pained, emotional, having fought this love, wanting to leave, to see the world, before taking her in his arms, giving in, giving up, melting into her. "Oh, *Mary, Mary,*" he whispers.

But that moment never came, much as I wanted it to. But, I think he really needed an adventure that I couldn't provide. And even more so, I sensed something deeper was at play. Involving God.

Then one day he announced he was making a move. To his place in the mountains. He'd maintain the cottage at the beach, but switch his base. He needed to get back to work and write and couldn't do it here with all the distractions. In the cabin, away from it all, he would.

I invited him for a drink, a kind of a goodbye. But we both knew it was our first real date, a progression. Same place, different hours. Different clothes. Different attitude. He was leaving. He felt safe. He actually told me that night, that he'd only fall in love at summer camp two weeks before he headed home. Short, full-blown affairs, with a guaranteed escape. This was his last two weeks. Camp was ending.

After a few beers, he confessed obliquely that he'd been tossed out of college. To this day, I'm not sure what happened, but I know it's something he lives with that lies heavy on his heart, that involved a woman and some frat brothers. Hookers? Wild Parties? Or something more serious? It was hard to tell. There is no way he'd ever hurt a woman – emotionally, I was to discover, all the time...but nothing more. You'd have to know him to understand my certainty. But he lives with something. The whole affair was mentioned, then quickly dropped, both of us wanting to move on to a happier note.

A few more beers and I confessed to a fantasy of making love in a bathroom of a restaurant in Paris. He was game.

Then, somewhere he managed to get in that he hurts people. Or was it that he's hurt people?

"But not me," I foolishly thought.

I know Mom. Another flag. A big one.

He walked me home, and as we stood on the bluff overlooking my house, I turned to say good night, and was met with a kiss. Barely a whisper. That would linger for days. I ran down the hill into the house and told David I was leaving. I was done. He'd been drinking and didn't say much.

But I had no idea where I was going, or how I was going to pay for it. The money I'd made over the last year had kind of magically appeared and allowed us to survive. But now, I needed a real job. A steady gig.

"They're looking for writers at The Division. Cop show, for Lifetime. Debra Levine is the Exec Producer. You know her?" I was on the phone with my agent a few days later.

Regrettably, I didn't.

"Every writer in town is up for the job." It was staffing season. *"All the other shows are full. It's your last shot."*

Sarah and I went in to pitch a story that we'd both discovered, independently, in newspapers, three thousand miles apart. A true story that was heartbreaking. An estranged father had wormed his way back into his ex's life under the guise of getting to know his two boys. He gave her a little money, a semblance of support. Things were looking up for this single over-worked mom and she began to relax, just a little. The guy had been a bum, but he seemed to have changed. He was coming through. Then he asked if he could take the boys camping, to bond, have some fun. Two days later he came back, alone, with a story. Said they'd wandered off while he slept. The search was on. On local TV he pleaded for their safe return. But his tale began to unravel just as the 2-year-old was found dead of exposure, and he was charged with murder. To add to the depravity of it all, in the courtroom he whispered to their mother as she passed to testify, that the other boy was still alive. That he had him, hidden. Taunting her. A real sicko. I took it and ran with it, twisting it further and pitched it to the show's creator and exec producer, a very cool cucumber. Hard to tell if she was impressed. And, as promised, it was a cattle call in there. Another team went in as we were leaving.

My agent told me we'd hear by the next day. I headed for the beach and into meditation, my second that day, and prayed. I knew I'd be leaving this world of joy and bliss and heading back into one of serial killers and rapists, and dirt and garbage, but I didn't care. I wanted to leave David and start over with Rio. Somehow, I would hold on to this other good stuff. This new world. This new way. But I needed money to do it. I wanted this job. "*I want it!*" I declared to the heavens and came out of meditation.

A haze had settled in around me. The day was hot, but the sun now obscured. As I got up and began to walk toward the pier and off the beach, I saw a man in the distance approaching, quickly. Headed straight at me. As he got closer I grew alarmed. He was small, no more than four feet, and hideous. For lack of a better description, he looked like a troll. The next thing I knew, we were face to face.

"If you had one wish, what would it be?"
was all he asked.
One wish.
I wanted this job, more than anything. To move on.
But I wanted Rio to be well.
I had to choose.
Tears came to my eyes.
"Do I have to tell you what I ask for?" I inquired.
"No," he said.
Well, heck, I'll ask for both, closed my eyes,
and silently did just that.
"Do you believe in miracles?" he asked when I finally opened them.
"Yes."
"You're a miracle."
"I'm a miracle," I added, far less convincingly.

That afternoon I got the call. The job was mine.

As for the second wish? The one about Rio being well?

That was more like wishful thinking.

That would take a miracle.

I take a guided meditation in a course I've signed up for. The meditation is a walk to God, at the end of which we're to ask a single question. Everyone closes their eyes and goes into the silence. We're to imagine a road. A structure up ahead. Traveling to it. Stepping in, you sense the Presence. Panic begins to set in. I'm new at this and getting nowhere. No connection. No Love. No structure up ahead. No Joy. Nothing.

God, you out there?
"Now ask the question," the moderator softly guides... "what question do you want to ask God?" Question? I'm not even on the friggin road. So, when the Balinese bell strikes, and everyone else opens their eyes and begins to scribble feverishly,
back into meditation I go, in a last-ditch effort. And immediately, shockingly, see a two-dimensional me, in miniature, on a small stage, walking on a dirt road, dressed like a Native squaw with Uggs on, the backdrop, a Rousseau-like painting, complete with a raccoon, a fox, and a bear peeking out from behind the bushes and trees. The whole thing a diorama, with me shuffling past. In the distance, up ahead, suspended in the sky, is a great castle, ablaze with light. Suddenly I'm inside the grand hall, yellow and white rays shooting everywhere. The light is blinding, illuminating a tower that goes upwards, forever. I try to ask my question, but promptly lose the connection. I journey back in, and after a few more failed attempts, I get the words out:
"Will Rio be well?"
And the answer comes:

"All is well in this place."

All is well in this place? All is well? For Rio? Where? What world are you living in? Cause it ain't well here. What are you saying? All is well. I didn't buy for a minute the crap some people fed me that the disabled are the ones who have it all, and we're the ones with the problem. I've witnessed too much of his pain. His loneliness. His frustration. I have all the respect in the world for the disabled. They function, they live our lives, the ones we bitch and moan about and screw up, and they do it all with a hundred-pound sack on their back. Try it some time. And you'll look at the disabled with the respect and awe they rightly deserve. But well? What are you saying? That everything is in some kind of Divine order? Perfect just as it is? I can't accept that. I won't accept that.

Or, that Rio's lot is Rio's lot. But for a few minutes a day, when he gets older he'll escape this debilitating disorder, in meditation? Find peace from the ticks? And the repetitive behaviors? And the nonsense, and the struggle? That he'll feel normal... In this place... for a few minutes a day... Is that what you're saying?

I'll take it.

Chapter 5
At Play in the Fields of the Lord

With the new job, suddenly there was enough money to make the move. It would still be tight. I'll be supporting David as well. He'd recently informed me he was coming after me for half my wages. He was legally entitled, but more than that, he was desperate.

Then he threatened to kill himself. His depression was as serious as his drinking, but he refused to get help. I finally told him that it was all his choice. It wasn't going to keep me there. So, he moved to Plan B, one final hurrah, pulling it together, driving into Beverly Hills to purchase a pair of diamond earrings for Christmas he knew I always wanted. With the money I needed to get out.

"When are you leaving David?" Jack asked, a slight impatience in his voice.

He never did make the move to Big Bear. We tried to separate from one another for a period after he casually mentioned he would probably marry the girl in Cuba. He wanted to buy property there. This would make it easier, if not possible.

"This is too crazy, even for me," I said and left.

But it didn't last. He wrote me a month later to come back. And I'd spent the whole time away missing him. Maybe he wouldn't leave. Maybe he couldn't leave. But, within a week of being back in his life, I felt awful. After I'd be with him, I'd feel drained. And after I saw him, depressed. I assumed it was because the relationship was going nowhere. Nothing had changed. It was Frank all over again.

I began to use my meditations more and more to lift me out of this funk. To lift my spirit, which had landed in a ditch somewhere. And while that had always brought me right back -- in fact meditation was beginning to be a panacea for just about everything -- for the first time, when I closed my eyes, it was filled with darkness. Like some great oil slick pitching laboriously from side to side on a rough sea, never lifting off. And I thought, love him or not, maybe I don't belong here. Maybe this darkness in my meditation is a message, direct from God. A warning. Now I felt both lousy and guilty. I opened my eyes and a surfer came out of the water. Those guys never talked to me, but this one, that day, said "hi."

"Hi," I replied, surprised. "How's the water?"

"Alright," he responded. "There's a cyclone in Alaska."

"Really? What's a cyclone in Alaska do to the water here?"

"Well," he explained, "with a typhoon you get lots of waves." "But with a cyclone, it just sort of sits there. Never lifts off."

Never lifts off? Maybe that's what was going on with my meditation! Maybe it's not Jack, I thought, delighted. Maybe I don't have to go. Say goodbye. Maybe it's the cyclone that's interfering with my meditation. Maybe it's not him. Maybe it's not God. Quickly forgetting all the rest... the other woman... his always leaving...

A week later I'm flat on my back, emotionally. I'm gettin' creamed.

Am I afraid of being alone? Truly alone? Is that what keeps me here? That fear? I'd heard a sermon on that, just the Sunday before. Our fear of being alone and the need to push through it. Like a crucifixion. To the other side. *"Should I leave him?"* I ask the universe in meditation. *"A simple answer, yes or no? That cyclone thing was a little confusing. So, should I leave?"*

"The answer to your question is yes."

I'm reading my horoscope under the glass, as I wait for my coffee the next morning.

"Stress independent thought and action.
There's a new kind of love
Waiting for you.
Rest assured you are not alone."

I stand there stunned. There was my answer. And a whole lot more. I was not alone. But wait a minute. What's this *"new kind of love"*??? "Waiting for me." What are we talkin' about? *As in, other-worldly?* As in, God? *Me and God, a thing?* I didn't like the sound of that one bit. I wasn't ready for a life in the convent.

But things with Jack went further south, fast. Then, he stopped coming to the beach altogether. Before Christmas, the Christmas of the diamonds, I saw him. He looked terrible. Barely recognizable. Like death. I was walking by the water with my best friend, and he jogged by in the opposite direction, just like the first day we met almost a year before. Only now, for him, it was as if we were strangers, as if none of it had happened. As he passed, I pulled his gift from my pocket and handed it to him. A small pewter coin engraved with an angel along with a silver heart. "Merry Christmas," I said. He thanked me and slowed, and looked down at them. "She looks like you. The angel."

Later, I looked down at another I had at home. He was right. She did.

The next time I saw him it was days before New Year's and he was headed back to Cuba, and her. Not completely well, but that wasn't going to stop him. I sat with him briefly on a bench outside the café. We chatted as if we were old acquaintances. He looked pretty awful. "Jungle fever. Again," he offered.

"You've lost your connection to God," I said. I don't know why I said it. I don't know what made me say it. It wasn't my language. I was still new at this. What did I know about connections? But something told me to say it. "Meditate," I told him, "every day. No kidding around."

"You really are an angel," he responded. And left to be with her.

But when he came back we started up all over again.

"When are you leaving David?" he asked, a slight impatience in his voice.

I moved out shortly after that, on Martin Luther King's birthday. I had a dream. "Free at last," Jack added, with what looked suspiciously like a smirk.

The year passed with magical mornings and an ever-deepening relationship with God. And more work than I knew what to do with, and love, both Divine and human. I'd wake up some nights to find light literally skipping over my body.

I wish you could hear the music I heard during that time. Or the sermons preached by Michael Beckwith at Agape at that moment. They were sheer inspiration. "My life is my message," I heard him say one Sunday, quoting Gandhi. In all my years of schooling, and I'd studied Gandhi more than once, I'd never heard those words.

"My life is my message."

Yes, his work as a pacifist and social organizer were his life. He lived it. Every day. Every moment. But I was beginning to think Gandhi was expressing something beyond that. At least, I was hearing something beyond that.

"My life is my message."

He became the message. His life became the message. He became the peace he sought. The love he sought. Not just some cause or bumper sticker.

My life is my message.

My life. How I live it every day. How I choose to express myself. Treat people. Spend my time. Who I am. That is my message. What a concept.

I thought my life was about making money. Marrying. Buying a house. Raising kids...Good kids. Sending them off to the best school they could get into. Watching them marry. The joy of grandkids. And getting old with someone. Retiring. Enjoying. Loving. Then, eventually, dying. All lived well. Even better, comfortably. Very comfortably. Isn't that what life is about? Isn't that what we're taught?

I was beginning to think there's far more going on here. A whole other story. A whole other journey.

I was happy on my own, flying free. Not a single regret. There was nothing about my marriage that I missed. You gotta' make happy memories to miss something. Something we'd failed to do.

And Rio was happy. He loved our new place. He had begun to show an interest, if not an autistic obsession in music. And all his favorite record labels were right around the corner of our sublet. For him, we were in heaven.

And Jack began to do the most beautiful artwork that would fall into place, was how he described the experience. Something was guiding him. But the work was uniquely him...his story. He was meditating every day. Connecting. And feeling great.

Only David was suffering. All semblance of a normal life, and structure, was gone. He was falling apart. At some point, Rio told me he didn't want to see his Dad anymore without my being there. Articulated with a clarity I had never seen. It had gotten to the point, where my greatest wish for him, was that at some time in his life he'd be able to go into a Starbucks and order a cup a coffee, and be understood. And not have people stare at him, or look away uncomfortably, as he struggled to get the words out.

But for a moment, a fleeting moment, he was making perfect sense. Like so many failed marriages, all the anger his father felt for me was being directed at him, and Rio was scared. I'd like to tell you I was sympathetic to David, but I wasn't. I put him on notice. Get a hold of your temper, or you'll never see him again. Things got better fast. After all, I was paying the bills. But more than that, way more than that, he loved Rio. If that were to happen, if I took him away... I think he would have killed himself.

About this time, Jack brought a good friend of his, another man, to meet me. "Can you do for him what you did for me?" he asked.

"It doesn't work that way," I answered. He's not my assignment. The truth is I could have, but I didn't know it back then. "I'm not in love with him," is what I wanted to say. "I don't want to spend every minute with him. Don't you get it?" My role as angel and woman completely blurred.

"He's like a magnet. We walk into bars and women flock to him in droves." This friend of Jack's tried to warn me. "I know where the bodies are buried."

But I wasn't dissuaded. By now, I had become a pretty serious student of all this, that which was happening to me, was reading everything I could get my hands on, and began to study. I wanted to understand it.... all of it. It was like I was being led through a magical story of love with Jack, with all its sizzle and intrigue, and heartache, and one with God, with all its beauty and love. Dividing my time pretty equally.

And I couldn't leave. Even knowing all this about him. It was like I was caught. Trapped. Hooked.

But she was always there. This polar-opposite of me. Now in addition to Big Bear and the ranch, there were trips to Cuba sprinkled in. One night, as we lay on his bed, Max between us, he alluded to a road he was on. Unsure of which way to go. He didn't come out and say caught between the two of us. Or that it may be a road leading to the dark, or the light, depending on the direction he took. No, just a road, leading in opposite directions. A photograph of a road, that road, that he'd just taken, stared back at us. Seemingly unrelated, he told me that night of a time when he worked as a bartender in Vegas, and over his head was that famous shot of Monroe from *Seven Year Itch*, her skirt being lifted by the draft of the train passing beneath her. She became a fantasy of his, he confessed, and when he hit L.A. he dated a Monroe look-a-like. Who stalked him when it was over. He wasn't sure that night why he was telling me this story. He's never told anyone. Just a road. Just a story.

But the next day he got a call, out of nowhere, from his ex-wife, tying the seemingly unrelated threads together. There was a script Monroe was set to do before she died, that was available. He should go after it. The title: "Something's Got To Give." He was bowled over by the coincidence and maybe got the meaning on some level. Something's got to give. "I know you're a gift from God," he'd also said that night. You don't pass up a gift from God, do you?

Apparently, you do, as he headed in the opposite direction, back to Cuba. But when he returned, he was in a foul mood and ill health, again. It appeared all was not perfect in paradise. Besides a painful hernia that hit midweek that I imagine put a serious crimp on all things sexual, I say smiling, he was beginning to suspect she was lying to him. She'd been elusive, disappearing for hours, showing up late, always with an excuse, a story. "Another man?" I asked, the completely objective observer. "A local?" It would be understandable. He still only went there a few times a year, for a week at a pop. And she was beautiful. A showgirl at the Tropicana I learn. Lead dancer. When he first told me she was a dancer, I just assumed he meant ballet and pictured Degas. Frankly, I didn't know which was worse. And all of twenty-eight. Waiting for him to make a move. "Or drugs?" I conjured further. "Maybe both," he answered coolly. But he was in no hurry to end it. He was as hooked as I was. Liar or not.

That night, unbeknownst to both of us, we went separately to a dinner party of a close friend of his, a wonderful painter who had now become a friend of mine as well. We were delighted to find each other there as dinner partners, and at some point, the host showed us a book that described the basis of his work. He randomly opened it to a page and I looked down to find a painting I'd seen 20 years before, part of an 'important' impressionist show that was touring the U.S. I was with David, still in the flush of early dating, and falling in love. He'd made reservations for this day of culture months before he knew that it would be the day of the big UCLA/USC game. His attention was lost somewhere between the game and the artwork, as play by play made its way through LACMA, the score traveling like a drumbeat to the members of its tribe. Meanwhile, I stood for a very long time before a fairly obscure small painting I'd fallen for, by a Swiss Artist, Felix Vallotton. The painting, circa late nineteenth century, was of a woman with a man, seductively leaning into him, whispering... melting. The work itself is pretty fantastic, but, as a storyteller, it was the title of the painting that got me: *The Lie*. I wondered as I stood there many years before, "What was the lie?" The story she was weaving-- whispering? Or the affair itself? Or both?

Now here it was showing up twenty years later. I was dumbstruck, considering the conversation we'd had that morning... and the question that hung in the air, "Was she lying?" I wondered if it was lost on Jack...this coincidence. I assumed it was, like all the others of late, dismissed. Or so I thought.

About a month later his behavior with me suddenly changed. He became more attentive. I looked up one day from meditation to find him on the pier, holding Max, waving his paw at me. And when I came off the beach another day he declared, "There she is. There's my girl. Full of light."

He took me to a screening and introduced me to more of his friends. Then, I asked him to a concert at the Getty. Some of the other writer/producers from the show were going. He agreed.

But I was on a script that weekend and never made it. I let him know and we switched the plan. We'd meet at the usual place. When I finally got there, he was talking to a girl standing nearby, the seat next to him empty.

"Well, it's about time you got here. He's been waiting. Wouldn't let anyone near it," she announced before she disappeared.

I slid onto the stool feeling adored, even if it came from her. Then, he yanked the chair closer and ordered me a beer. And somewhere got in that he'd left her --- the girl from Cuba. It was over. We'd finally have a chance to play out all this feeling that had built up for more than a year. That resulted that night in a kiss that lasted for hours. And a hunger for each other that I'd never experienced. Before drifting off to sleep, wrapped in his arms.

"That was beautiful," he said the next morning as I left. "Really beautiful."

And it was.

I was floating. On my way to drowning.

"I'm sorry, Yahweh"

In a dream, my sister's brought me to the Queensboro Bridge in New York. "Judy, Judy, come you've got to see!" And as I stood on the railing, perfectly balanced, my arms outstretched at my sides, defying both logic and gravity, I looked up through the triangular grid of iron as the light fell, and the sky turned a beautiful deep blue, the stars aligning in that message:

"I'm sorry, Yahweh"

Yahweh? Hardly a word in my vernacular. Not even a word I knew. The holiest name of God, I learn. So holy it could never be spoken. An apology to God. From me? For what? Which transgression? This one? For this?

In the dream we're divided into four groups and have two weeks to say goodbye to people we'll never see again.

Chapter 6
The Wolf

There once was a man long ago, who told a story of two dogs.
One was very kind, the other ferocious and cruel. At times the
tension between them would erupt into a bloody battle.
Fearing the worst, he erected a fence, keeping them apart.
But one day the voracious wolf of a dog escaped,
and attacked. It was a fight to the death.

"Who won?" someone called out from the crowd.

"Whichever one I fed."

"It's never gonna happen again. Not in this lifetime."

I'd asked him if he would get tested. This was his response. Our lovemaking had fallen just short of intercourse. I hadn't had a period in over a year, but that morning, before our night together, it arrived, like some fertility rite that first day of Spring, keeping us apart. By the next day, it was gone, never to return. God? The thought certainly crossed my mind, but for the moment I had to get out of the way of the Mack truck that was about to run me over.

"It's not gonna happen. It's not in my heart."

Not in his heart? His words had the desired effect, cutting right through me. Crushing me. I knew he had pushed other women away in the past. Other wives. Had run from them. He'd even warned me. "I hurt people." But my head was reeling. And my heart was breaking. And I forgot all of that rational stuff in this pain, feeling the full weight of his rejection.

"I feel like I've betrayed her," he went on to say.

"Betrayed her?" I blurted out.

What about me? We'd been inseparable, rain or shine. I'd never experienced a betrayal like this. It took everything in me not to throw my iced coffee in his face. He said how much he appreciated that I was trying to understand, rather than just walk away.

And I was trying. Why would someone throw away something this extraordinary? This magical? Somehow I got through it – we got through it. But as much as I tried to find a way to stay, it grew worse. He was making it impossible. He was on and off. Lovely one day, then cold and unfeeling the next. The magic was still there when he'd allow it, and talk of God and our respective dreams, that I was somehow able to understand. But more and more, the conversation between Jack and his friend who owned the café grew dark. They would debate who was more evil, Hitler or Stalin, as if either's actions could be justified. Or running whores in Costa Rica. Or making hurtful references to the girlfriend in Cuba, who was now back on, stronger than ever. I got the feeling that if the curtain were lifted, there'd I'd be, angel me, perched on a rock surrounded by demons. Entertaining them. Like some twisted Wendy. Not admitting I was their prisoner. His prisoner.

I tried to understand. I meditated and prayed. Take this feeling away. This pain. Take my feelings away. Take me away. Break whatever spell was keeping me there. That I thought was love. It was Frank all over again....only much worse.

This wasn't love. This was the exact opposite. The withholding of love. Likely, something he learned at the hands of his mother. Wanting me to feel as badly as he had. Punishing me. I began to believe that one's journey – the story they're living – begins in childhood. That the events of that time, those early years, are clues to the journey you're on in this lifetime. He once remarked that sometimes it's impossible to break free of those early events. That one gets caught there, unable to move on, running in circles.

But all that understanding didn't matter. It was devastating.

In direct contrast to what I was receiving in meditation from God. God had no problem loving me. He thought I was kind of swell. Had thought fit to wake me up, for whatever reason – whatever good I had done to deserve this love that poured through me every day still remained a mystery. A love that celebrated me, not one that made me feel inadequate. Or constantly auditioning for a role it was becoming abundantly clear I was never gonna get. Not at my age, competing with a twenty-eight-year-old Cuban showgirl. Not for him. The artist/adventurer and the native showgirl. All very Hemingway, and no doubt very sexy. No contest.

And more and more the culture around me reflected his choice, as billboard after billboard sprung up beckoning the rider to pull off at that next gentlemen's club. And white girls, if not nice girls, fell out of favor, as rap went mainstream and introduced its idea of beauty into our culture. Black. Hispanic. Anything, but white. And Sex. Raunchy, out there, in your face, sex. "I'm in love with a stripper," the singer crooned on Kiss-FM as I drove Rio to school. Then, later, "Suck my lollipop." "I can make your bed rock." Just for starters. It was as if the world was becoming a reflection of his choice, his mind. More and more I felt like I was living in Frank Capra's *Wonderful Life*, only it's Pottersville, and George indeed had never been born.

A few more days in hell, and I know I have to go. Have to leave him. I used to love to stand directly behind him, in his shadow, and feel his energy on me. "You have a king in you," I tell him as I leave, "The energy of a king. But your lower self is a real son of a bitch."

I climbed into my SUV and started it up. The radio came on, to a station I'd never heard before. Had no idea how it got there, but I was riveted. It was a story of a rape. And a group of men who'd perpetrated it long ago. I sat there and listened, transfixed. It was his story. Only it was the Bible, circa 1100 B.C. The opening verses of the first book of Samuel. The story of Saul.

When I got home, I hit the computer. And I began to read. And what I found was a tale to rival *Game of Thrones*.

There'd been a rape, a brutal gang rape. And the girl – a concubine of a holy man (ponder that one) -- was left to die. The men of her tribe declared war on the tribe of Benjamin, where the crime had occurred, slaughtered every man, their women married off to others.

Generations later, the tribes of Israel were threatened by a vicious enemy. They needed to unify to stand a chance, to save themselves from a gruesome torture and death. They wanted a king that would bring them together. Someone who could save them. But God refused. "There will be no king," he said. No king before me. Nothing between us. But they insisted. And through his prophet Samuel, God warned them: He will take your sons into battle, this king, and he will take your money. But they wouldn't listen. So, he gave them Saul.

Saul. The best lookin' guy in town. Heads above everyone else, literally. Of the tribe of Benjamin. That same tribe that so long ago had been disgraced by a gang rape. How surprising that God would choose this tribe to pick the first King. But for my money, Saul seemed like a good choice, great choice even. Strong guy, great fighter; definitely the guy you want on your team when you head into war. A guy's guy, a man's man. And indeed, he saves the people from their gruesome fate. But then, it seems, defies the word of God. He goes into battle without waiting for the prophet, Samuel, to offer the blessing, rather performing it himself. No big deal in my book. And frankly the more I read, the more I'm dubious of this prophet Samuel. He seemed to me equally part pious, and more than part filled with his own ambition and self-importance, self-interest. I don't trust him. No doubt this new king was cutting into his role as mediator with God. The whole matter, the charge leveled against Saul, seemed much ado about nothing.

And, in fact, it is Saul's second act that costs him the throne. Against the order of God, he fails to kill the King of the Amalekites. The Amalekites, I learn, are a pretty nasty bunch. It appears when the Israelites were fleeing Egypt and hit the Red Sea and the waters miraculously parted, these guys – the Amalekites -- picked off anyone who fell behind – slaughtered them: the sick, the feeble, the elderly, the children. The most vulnerable. Not for the Egyptians -- no, just for the thrill of the kill. Nice guys. And a pure hatred of Israel. Like I said, nasty bunch. And for this reprehensible act, Saul is told by God to eliminate this nation -- men, women, children, flora, fauna, the whole megillah. Nothing should remain. Not a speck. Forget the fact that this is the kind of talk that gives the God of the Old Testament a bad name. That doesn't appear to be an issue for Saul, the root of his hesitation. To the contrary. Saul had no problem killing innocent children or -women but only defies the order as it relates to their king, Agag. He allows him to survive, along with the choicest cattle, both of which he brings home with him.

Spoils of war? Perhaps. It seems it was the custom of the day for the victor to parade the vanquished through the streets as further humiliation. A tradition by the way, that survives to this day. We were treated to just this sort of frightening spectacle in Iran, circa 1972. Or, in the videos released by terrorist organizations of the 'condemned' journalist or soldier. Or, on our part, the public hanging of

Saddam Hussein. Perhaps that's what Saul was planning before he killed him. But no such plan existed.

To me, allowing Agag to survive represented Saul's inability, as a king of this world, to kill another just like him. That he held a certain reverence for him, regardless of Agag's, and his people's, cruelty. And something about Jack is giving me a window into Saul.

Saul's refusal to kill Agag not only cost him the kingdom, but God departed from him as a result of this defiance, and Saul began a very different kind of journey, into paranoia, rage, and madness. And David, the "great" king David, husband of Bathsheba, father of Solomon, is chosen to be his successor at his death.

And Agag? Well, he met his fate at the hands of old Samuel the prophet, who promptly beheaded him, but not before Agag sired a son, continuing the line of this enemy of Israel, that would rear its ugly head again....and again. That story, I was to discover, much to my surprise, was far from over.

Then, Saul's son Jonathan catches my attention, as he drifts between his father and David, as the deadly competition between the King and his successor heats up. Jonathan warns David of his father's plan to murder him, despite the family ties, for Jonathan and David loved each other more than a man and a woman.[3] (The friendship was so affectionate and loving, I even ran into more than one commentator, albeit untraditional ones, who speculated that possibly, they were gay.) But in the end, Jonathan chooses to

---

[3] "How I weep for you, my brother Jonathan! Oh, how much I loved you! And your love for me was deep, deeper than the love of women!" 2 Samuel 1:26

die by his father's side in battle, a father who more than once had tried to kill him, his own son, as well.

And then, it hit me. My father's name is Saul. And I was to be Jonathan if I'd been a boy. And my Hebrew name is Bathsheba. And I'm married to David. Was it...could it... all be just coincidence?

The more I read about Saul, the more it sounds like Jack. The mood swings, the hero, the remoteness, the quality of the king, and yes, the cruelty. But something else, something I couldn't explain, beyond a cognitive recognition of any similarity. It was a feeling that as I was reading about Saul, I was reading about Jack. And it was my knowing Jack that was my way into Saul. That made him so real. Come alive. To live this story. Be in the midst of it.

And the more I read about David, the more it reminded me of my own husband. The promise of a great young man, who would later retreat into his own narcissism. The arrogance and pompousness. Dancing naked in the streets. Cavorting in the wilderness as he fled Saul, picking up wives along the way. Callously putting others in danger, as he satisfied his own needs. I read of Michal, Saul's daughter, David's first wife, who he abandoned as he fled Saul. Michal, who loved David. Who saved him from the first of her father's murderous plots, warning him of the soldiers who were on their way. Lowering him from the window, covering for him, lying for him. A woman, and wife, who David quickly forgot in the ensuing years on the run. Then cruelly ordered back to join his entourage of wives at the palace, notwithstanding the fact she'd found happiness in a marriage to another. What did he care when his ego was at stake? A woman he never spoke to again after she challenged that ego, that narcissism. But still, he kept her there.

As I made my way deeper into the story, the more I wondered, why God was so tolerant of this man? Who orchestrated the death of Bathsheba's husband to cover up his own sexual indiscretion? Did nothing when his own daughter Tamar is brutally raped and discarded by her stepbrother? And finally, ordering the death of another son, Absalom, who reacted in rage at his father's failure to avenge that rape? The list of David's ills goes on, and on. Why is God so accepting of David as compared to the short leash he has Saul on?

And then there's Jonathan, caught between these two men, relinquishing any right to the throne, as the eldest son of Saul, in favor of God's chosen, David. Seemingly selfless. Loving David, but aligned and attached to his father. To death.

Then, in one of the readings on Saul, I saw the word parchment, highlighted, and remembered Jack's early dream.

"It was my writing," he said, *"but it was your Spirit that was infusing my words. The paper was brown parchment, but the writing was silver and gold."*

And immediately clicked on:

"A sumptuous form of parchment was produced at an early date by dyeing the material a rich purple and lettering it in

silver and gold. The purple dye was subsequently abandoned, but the practice of "illuminating" parchment manuscripts in gold and silver flourished."[4]

I sat there, dumbfounded. Wondering what it all meant. What was it trying to say? Was this story playing out in my life somehow? This myth. Was I carrying it? Where David is David. And Jack is Saul. And I, the feminine Jonathan caught between the two? Were these the archetypes that Jung writes about? Characters, patterns, stories, symbols that we all carry in the unconscious. Contained in us all, regardless of our heritage or lineage, or tribe? That show up in our dreams. Animate our lives, without our knowing. Unconsciously informing our decisions, our actions. *"Each of us"*, Joseph Campbell writes, *"has an individual myth that's driving us, which we may or may not know."* [5] Is this that myth? In my life?

Is it possible that we're carrying that story? Their story? Had these archetypes – the brooding murderous king, the anointed successor, the humble mediator in love, drifting between them -- somehow come alive in us? Could this in some odd way explain the golden blanket of the wedding morning? Of our marriage being blessed? This union of "David" and "Jonathan"?

And the more I read about the prophet Samuel, full of piety, but equally full of himself and his own self-

---

[4] http://www.britannica.com/EBchecked/topic/443382/parchment

[5] Joseph Campbell, "Pathway to Bliss", p.87

importance, the more it reminded me of David's roommate at Yale, Joe Lieberman.

I couldn't wait to tell Jack, the details literally pouring out of me. What did it all mean? Could this be why we're so connected? Why leaving him is near impossible, even for a day? For him, we finally had a way to relate, that was safe.

"You're my son," he concluded.

Funny, I never felt anything like this for my father.

Then, the Bible showed up again. A seatmate on a plane heading east shared he was doing his thesis on the story of Abraham and Sarah and Hagar. The horror of 9/11 was still fresh in our minds. Did I understand the relevance of this story? The relationship to those events? I didn't know the story, I confessed. My total knowledge of the Bible was The Saul and David affair (which, by now, I had researched fairly extensively) and whatever knowledge I had picked up and retained from childhood tales told in Hebrew School, a step up from Golden Books. Or popular culture. I mean, who doesn't know about the flood? Or a birth in a manger? And, thanks to Hollywood, a respect for Moses? But Abraham and Sarah and Hagar? Certainly no one was covering the events of the Twin Towers from a biblical angle, short of a blip I subsequently ran across on NPR. But, as soon as I got home, I looked into it.

I read how Sarah had laughed when she overheard the angel tell Abraham that he and his wife were to bear a child. Can't blame her, a young beauty at ninety. How she had given Abraham her handmaiden, Hagar, to give him that son in her place doubting God's word, when her own pregnancy didn't follow. It was Abraham who was to bear the son, she concluded, not her. That's what God meant. An act of disbelief that resulted in the birth of a child named Ishmael. But after Hagar conceived, she turned on Sarah, taunting her, belittling her, acting superior to her, as the mother of Abraham's unborn child. Sarah pleaded with her husband for help. Whatever you want, darling, he said, do whatever you please. Ultimately Abraham sent Hagar and Ishmael away to die in the desert, rejecting them. But God intervened and saved the woman and child, and from this son, I learn to my utter surprise, the Nation of Islam is born. All from Sarah's doubt of the word of God, the will of God, the promise of God. That gave rise to the rejected son. That Jung would call the shadow, the rejected aspect.

And he will be a wild man; his hand will be against every man,
and every man's hand against him;

Genesis 16:12

Then, I read of the subsequent birth to Abraham and Sarah of Isaac, who would give birth to Jacob and the nation of Israel and the Judea/Christian faith. Two nations perpetually at war. One now seeking to annihilate the other. And all of this in the Bible?

Could Campbell be right that we're always living myths? That we just don't know it? Could this be that myth? Is this story at play? At the root, the true heart of this modern-day conflict? Literally, its genesis? Had we gotten so blind, so ignorant of these stories, so arrogant even, that we fail to recognize them as they unfold before our very eyes? I certainly was. Had the Bible become off limits in our secular world? Was it so discredited that it ranked about on par with a fairy tale? Once upon a time...[6] It certainly had for me. Just stories of a lot of tribes and wars, and kings who drew God's wrath when they turned to worship idols with meaningless names. Stories whose relevance in my own Faith was reduced to our history. Our suffering. Our distinction. And in the Christian faith from what I could tell from the Radio, a book with stories that serve in their meaning as the absolute truth and a moral guide to living. In fact, the only guide. As well as historical fact. But a living myth playing out right now? Right in front of me? Demanding my attention?

Off the story of Abraham, I begin to read about his nephew Lot, made rich by the gifts of God, but who can't resist "facing his tent toward Sodom," ultimately moving into the gates of this prurient place. As Jack leaves again for Cuba. To his fantasy. He's begun to send her three hundred a month, and for that he's tied to her and tied her. Bought her. She's his. While he's away, our myths cross in a dream.

In the dream, I'm trying to get to him. I know it's a dream because I'm a great jogger (only in dreams, regrettably) and I look terrific in a pair of short-shorts and a tank top (even more regrettable, the only in a dream part). I'm running towards his house, to him. But as I set out, I see the upper portion of a very large thick snake, a cobra, sticking out of the

---

[6] Not for a moment minimizing the psychological substance and significance of those stories known as fairytales.

sand, directly in front of where we sit every day at the café. It's purple in color, a good four feet of it showing, its eyes set off by a set of thick, false lashes. They're her eyes. It's her, the girl from Cuba. A snake.
As I approach she warns me that I'm not getting by. That he's hers. All hers. Undaunted, I keep running. She reiterates the warning. "Don't even think about it." But I'm just as determined to get to him. Suddenly, she shoots up in the air, all eight feet or more, and flies right at me. I take off, shooting through the galaxy, my first and only flight in a dream, she literally on my tail. A scene right out of Star Wars. That ends with me lying in the arms of God,
like a babe in some Henry Moore sculpture, it's massive marble arms enveloping me, its face out of frame, a Buddha-like smile on my own. Safe and warm. And I hear the voice of God declare:

"All there is, is God. There is no snake."

Wait a minute. No snake? No evil? What are you saying? That it's all an illusion, as the Hindus believe? The Maya? Vishnu's dream? Dreaming us? That we're all just souls sitting up there, above the klieg lights, staring down at the stage below? Watching this drama, we call our lives, play out? That the world is indeed a stage, as Shakespeare once said? And we're its players?

Or, that there is no snake. Only God. Just God. That it's all God, the snake, the "enemy", all of it. That it's God leading me, chasing me, into the arms of God. Certainly, her presence in my life, and his life, has lead me running to God in the pain it's causing. In my feelings of inadequacy. Of rejection. Is that her purpose? Is that his? Are we all God?

Could that be the purpose of all this? Of 9/11? Had our worship of money, of this tallest building as Campbell so eloquently revealed, replaced any concept of God? Had we found security and placed our faith in our 401(k)s? And house values? Had they become our idols? Our "gods"? Overtaken any belief in something Divine? Any desire to know it? Or even knowledge that it existed? Had for me. Could these other gods – these tallest buildings -- be coming down? I mean, literally? Could God, as in the endless stories of the Old Testament, be once again using a so-called "enemy" to bring us back to him? A financial collapse to bring us back to him? As he brought Israel back to him, through famine, countless enemies, countless times? Is it all taking us, chasing us, back to God? Is that its purpose? As pews fill in the aftermath of 9/11?

Could these ancient stories have great meaning, beyond history, martyrdom, moral lessons? Could we actually be living them, right now?

Is it all God?

I'm beginning to think the answer is yes.

2

The

Miracle

Chapter 7

Hey Jude

I move again. This time to the beach. A two-story affair with vaulted ceilings, wood beams and 26-foot windows, just south of the Venice Pier, that looks out on the very spot of my awakening, and the wish from the troll. Where Jack, Max, and I meet every morning. And where from an enormous deck I watch the sun set, and the lights of the pier come on every night. It's heaven.

I didn't move in right away. I want it to be ready and furnished for Christmas, to surprise Rio, with a tree right out of the Nutcracker in the middle of the room, that climbs to fill this magical cavern of a space. Then, one night, shortly after I get the key, I head down there at three a.m., panicked that I'd left the heat on earlier that day. The beach was blanketed in a thick fog, and, as I approached, I could hear a fog horn in the distance, calling. It was pure magic, and I wonder, what am I waiting for? We pack our bags and move in the next day, a couple of mattresses thrown down on the floor.

My life is sweet. I can see the water glistening on the ocean from my bed, once I finally get one. At dusk, lights twinkle on ships from distant lands, and a mist shrouds the mountains. I feel like I'm living in Valhalla.

"I have Christ in me"

I hear this in a dream, shortly after I make the move. No visuals, no frills, no story, just these words... that thought. Despite my Semitic roots, I instinctively know what it means. That something, called the Christ, is living in me.
Has awakened in me.
That a consciousness has activated. The Christ. The Messiah. And I figured all this out just as soon as I realize that Christ was not Jesus' last name.

Still, I find it odd that I would dream in a language that had been an anathema to my family and faith. You didn't mention Jesus, or the concept of Christ in my house, as if he was some traitor to the cause, to his people. And for sure, the Inquisition didn't help. And still, whenever Michael Beckwith cautiously introduced the concept of the Holy Spirit into an otherwise metaphysical sermon, you could hear the congregation bristle, Jew, Catholic, Buddhist, lapsed Christians, alike, including me. For so many, Church had been a miserable experience of hell and damnation. And Guilt. And sin. For me, language like the Holy Spirit or Christ Consciousness was Christianity not so cleverly disguised.

So, given all that, I find it interesting that the dream spoke in these terms. That it didn't say the Messiah, or considering what I was reading, the Buddha, the Tao, the Atman presence, Universal life force, Infinite Intelligence, Divine Love, anything... No, it said "Christ". As in, "I have Christ in me."

I wondered what Tim would say, the towheaded cheerleader at high school so many years ago, who told me I was headed for hell for not accepting Jesus Christ as my personal savior.

The wind blows where it wishes

I read these words in a Jungian work citing the book of John, my introduction to the New Testament:

No one knows where it comes from or where it goes.
So it is with everyone who is born of Spirit.

John 3:18.

As it was with me. The Wind... Spirit... found me out of nowhere. Landed on me that first day, and filled me with joy. A gift. Of Grace. And no one was asking me to accept anyone as my personal savior as a condition for any of this, as far as I could tell.

All it was asking, I came to discover, was my time and my attention, my desire, my heart, my love, my life. A willingness to let go of this world, to turn away. Tall order.

But the truth is, since my awakening, I've lost my taste for the things of this world. That is my spoiler alert. If you seek this you will never see this world, or desire the things of it, quite the same. Oh, I still love a good steak. And a cocktail. And the smell of Jasmine in the Spring. And most of all the ocean, each and every day of the week. And being in love. But now all of it is brought to me by Spirit, an energy that is turning everything, every day on its head and enchanting it. All of it.

"Why not heal Rio?"

The thought suddenly occurs to me one day. And reading that still makes me cry.

Why not? Ever since this wind blew into my life, everything has changed. The struggle's gone. It's all begun to unfold, magically, if not always magnificently. Everything but Rio. His struggle, if anything, is getting worse. More and more I'm covering for him in conversations. Filling in the gaps. Prompting him to stay on point. Helping him to make sense. And he's becoming more isolated and ever more rigid. More compulsive. Crying over any change in his routine. Arguing with other kids. Spacing out. We have him on medication and once we get it right, a disastrous four doctors later, and find the incomparable Skip Baker, some of that improves. But the tics get worse. And for the first time, he seems like the other kids in his special day class. Autistic. I watch him at the graduation party from his elementary school, standing in the water alone, talking to himself. Playing like a baby....at eleven. Even in this group of disabled children, he seems unable to keep up with their boogie boards and body surfing. And the most recent testing has revealed he may never mature, a finding the psychologist is trying to get me to accept. No problem for her. And, the prospects look dim that he'll ever express himself with any depth, or comprehend an abstract thought. Or know where to begin a task, a test, a chore. Or pour a drink. Or button his pants. Or make a meal. Heck, a sandwich. Or cut his food. Or wash his face.

But, in the last year or so, he's taught himself to read, through the fine print of the liner notes in the CDs he's begun to collect. Obsessively collect. Every Friday night we head out to Tower Records, where he selects a new CD or two, to celebrate the week-- his week -- his victories. We're only too delighted to do this... to celebrate each accomplishment. The use of a word... an understanding... anything... everything. It's made us appreciate it all. To see moments that would have gone unnoticed, if things had been normal. Then, off for pizza and a frozen yogurt. On the way, he'd hand each CD for me to open....a minor freak-out if it didn't have the lyrics, and jubilation if it did. Then, meticulously he'd begin the ritual of running his finger over every line. I'd hear the screech of his nail as it went across the page from the backseat. He'd spend hours this way, buried in the minutia, pouring over the thank-you's, the credits. Little did I know he understood what he was reading. Books had eluded him. But, something that interested him endlessly, to the point of obsession, taught him to read. At the age of nine.

"I want to be in the music business."

Who said that? I follow the voice to my son perusing the bins one such Friday night in search of something he'd heard on Radio Disney, a self-imposed obsessive prerequisite that denies him hundreds of artists he truly wants. But the ritual's got a momentary hold on him that he can't break.

"You wanna' work here?" I ask.

I struggle with every word, hating the thought of it, still caught in my middle-class dreams for him. Trying to lower my expectations as I had been advised by his doctors that week, after a blistering dressing down based on new testing, and an order to get real. That those expectations I had for him were unfair....to him. That the language I used when speaking to him, was all but incomprehensible. Way beyond his reach. I had to change.

And knowing full well that his functioning even here, working retail, was a ridiculous suggestion. An impossibility.

Still, he shoots me a look and quickly sets me straight.

"I wanna' be a rapper. And own my own label.
You gotta dream bigger than that, Mom"

Tears came to my eyes. He was right. Under doctor's orders I'd taken that dangerous step away from dreaming at all. And he got it all out with a clarity I'd only seen once before. About David. Here it was again. A glimpse of Rio without Autism. Before lapsing back into the struggle.

Why not heal him? Now there's a big dream.

But, I had no idea where to begin. I confide my desire to my closest friend. She's completely on board, no hesitation. She thinks the idea is brilliant, which is why I love her so, and suggests I go into meditation and ask if anyone wants to help. The *anyone*, I presume is an angel or two. She's very strong on fairy magic, likely because she is one.

Despite my increasing biblical roots, and an affinity to a one God concept, I go for it. Use her script. Follow her plan. Go into meditation.

> *"I want to heal my son," I call out to the universe.*
> *"Does anyone want to help me?"*

Three weeks later I'm on my deck at sunset, thinking about the events of that morning. I'd been tied up with Rio, and my time with Jack was a quick drive-by. He walked to the car and asked Rio through the open window, how Luthifer was, our escape artist of a hamster. Had we found him? he inquired. "Luther," Rio laughed. And in his garbled way got out that he was still gone and then added, "Mommy thinks the place is magic."

"Oh, God my mother's gonna kill me," I thought, as I sat on the deck later that day. It's bad enough that he's ostracized because of the autism. Now he's talking magic.

Then suddenly, I heard a voice – more like a series of thoughts coming clearly through me.

*"Use magic to get Rio to meditate, and meditate with him every day,
and he will be healed."*

I burst into tears.

*"And make a movie about it…
Cause the world needs to see a miracle right now."*

Then, a forgotten horoscope from that morning, barely glimpsed at the coffee shop, flashes through my mind, word for word. One that I hadn't paid attention to, until now, as it suddenly floods my consciousness:

"You're about to witness what appears to be a miracle. But it may be an illusion."

Oh, the universe is so clever, I thought, laughing. It's all a bloody illusion.

Then I sat for a long time and watched as the sun set and thought about the words I'd just heard… let them really sink in. "He will be healed." There I go again. Little Miss Waterworks. Even now. Then, I thought of my father for some reason. And all the implications, as my excitement grows.

"I have to get a video camera for the movie," I think as I head downstairs.

In the bathroom, I hear the voice again.

"Get back on the roof. We're not done."

I did.

"Rio wants to make a movie about Sgt. Peppers. Make the movie and by the time you're finished, he will be healed."

Rio had this idea about a week or so before. "*Who are the people,*" he asked from the backseat of the car, "*on the cover of Sgt. Pepper's?* "*How did the Beatles pick them...?*" "*Wouldn't that make an interesting documentary?*" It took about twenty minutes to get all that out. When I turned around I saw he was looking at the artwork on the CD. It was a great idea. Who were those people? And why did the Beatles pick them? These lonely hearts.

Then, I promptly got caught up in life and work, and relegated it to that mental file of great notions lived out, or not, sometime in the future.

Now it's coming up again. Get a camera and begin research. The checklist in my head is growing. Then, my mind wanders as I begin to think again of Rio being healed. And all the people who had worked with him who would be so thrilled.

And I think of Dr. Bill.

Bill Takesheta is an extraordinary man and genius who came into our life and informed us that Rio wasn't seeing. Well, not exactly. He could see, but he had no visual perceptual skill. As I understood it, it was like a blind person who suddenly gets sight, but has no idea what he's looking at. To determine this, Bill had placed a turquoise wood triangular block above a yellow wooden square to make a house. Then, asked Rio to build his own, with the identical blocks set out before him. Rio tried, struggled, even jammed the two together, but for the life of him could not make the blocks look like Bill's. And had no idea how to make that happen. Tears came to my eyes as I watched. I could feel his frustration. Bill finally gave him a verbal clue, "Rio, put the triangle on top of the square." And Rio did just that, sandwich-like, one on top of another. Bill took Rio on as a patient and worked with him tirelessly, patiently, four days a week that summer. For no money. We were at war with the insurance company as it was, and this was cutting edge stuff. They ultimately kicked in and we paid Bill the six thousand or so that was our share. But he never asked for it. Not once. We continued to see him once a week, for a number of years. The progress had been slow. Rio still struggled to complete even the simplest puzzle. And he worked on what Bill called executive planning, the ability to mentally break down a task, to know where to begin. All of this continued to be out of Rio's reach. But there had been victories. He was slowly getting better, thanks to Bill, this angel, who had treated the blind and partially blind all his professional life. Who had helped Rio to learn *to see*. And who went blind over Christmas, over a period of three weeks, at the age of forty-two. And off all this, I heard the final thought:

"Bill gave Rio his sight. Rio's gonna give Bill back his."

I race to the coffee shop and spot the horoscope still under the glass, the words exactly as I had heard them on the roof.

"You're about to witness what appears to be a miracle."

"Sure, take it," the night guy offers from behind the counter.

I do, as the opening lines of "Hey Jude" fill the space, adding another layer of magic and meaning. Jude, an affectionate diminutive of my own name that I've always loved. Here it was now, calling me.

From a machine outside of the liquor store, I grab the last copy of the local morning paper Jack would have read to me, the one I'd missed that morning, and head into our place, on the oft chance he'll be there. I was so excited I wanted to share all of this with him. I ordered a beer and opened the paper to the horoscopes. And found what I hadn't been there earlier to hear:

*"There's always a way to work things out — something you believe
to your very core.
You're very inspiring when you turn creative fantasies
into artistic projects.
A child is the focus of some special effort."*[7]

---

[7] Joyce Jillson, *The Daily Breeze*, February 15, 2003, B6.

I was dumbfounded, again, rushed home and called my mother. Told her everything.

"Next thing I know you're gonna tell me you're Mary." Her voice is skeptical and amused, with a tinge of mock disbelief.

"I'm not Mary, mother," feeling slightly deflated, but refusing to give in. "But isn't it exciting?" I wanted to get the attention off of me, to where it belonged. If not on something Divine, then at the very least, the thought of Rio being healed.

"Yes," she finally conceded, "it's all very exciting... if it works. You know it's your father," she immediately added. "He told me that if God grants him a wish in heaven, it will be for Rio." That she could believe. And who's to say she isn't right? I had thought of my father.

Later, snuggled into bed in my castle on the water, I picked up my copy of Marianne Williamson's *Return to Love*, opened it, and my eyes went to the exact spot where I'd left off the night before:

"And when the angels awakened Mary in the middle of the night, they told her to meet them on the roof."[8]

Just as I'd heard... The roof... The upper room... The higher consciousness... Get back on the roof.

---

[8] Marianne Williamson, A Return to Love, (Harper Perennial, 1992) p.294

"Use magic to get him to meditate."

I followed the instructions and started with Rio the very next morning, with a story I conjured about Harry Potter and how this would be even better than that. Then, we looked out thru the wall of windows at the ocean, my ocean, and I invited him to see the presence of God, everywhere, that had become so easy for me to see. To see it. Really see it. And feel it. In the waves. In the birds that flew over. In the sky. Knowing that God is everywhere. And if God is everywhere, then God is where you are, where I am, right now. Then, we closed our eyes. I think I chanted a little, a few phrases I'd picked up along the way, "God only, only God, God only, only God. Right here right now God is, right here, right now Love is, Peace is, Joy is, Rio is, I am." And then went silent. We only sat there for a few minutes, as I felt the Presence activate within me. Then I heard myself speak a healing, borrowing heavily from Michael Beckwith. That the presence of God was moving through Rio, healing everything that needs to be healed. Every cell. Every corpuscle. That neurotransmitters are firing. That new neural pathways are happening right now! Synapses, synapsing! Cylinders clicking into place! I could feel it. I could see them. And declared it. That things...That his handwriting is better....and easier for him now! I heard my voice rising. Giving profound thanks. Knowing it was already done in the mind of God.

I didn't know if the prayer had any effect. The voice had only said to meditate. But something impelled me to throw it in. For good measure? I have no idea. These were unfamiliar waters, to say the least.

But almost immediately the tics began to disappear. The repetitive speech. That first week, David got three phone calls from different doctors and therapists. Rio was doing great. Doing things that had stymied him for years. Thrown a ball overhand for the first time, at age 12, and hit an 'x' on the wall! Four weeks later he was sitting in standardized testing, with an aide. Moving through the test, answering the questions. Maybe not all right, but he knew where to begin! David was elated when he dropped him off after cognitive therapy. Rio had been amazing! Giving answers, doing puzzles! I finally told him what had happened. What I was doing. He cut me off and told me I was crazy. That none of this had anything to do with me or God. That the timing was just coincidence. That all the therapies he'd arranged were finally kicking in. Paying off. I reminded him of a conversation he'd had with me only two weeks before. That he could no longer watch Rio at this same cognitive therapy. That it was too painful. He had mimicked Rio's frustrated attempts. He didn't mean to be cruel, but I couldn't watch. Now David was beaming and my news was destroying his elation. I promptly let it go.

A week later I ask for a sign. Is this really happening… this healing? Or is David right? That it's all just coincidence? That it is the years of therapy finally paying off. Not God. I didn't doubt the miracle, or God's hand in it for one minute, but I wanted to be sure I hadn't gone clear off the rails. Give me a sign, God. Let me know.

David dropped Rio off later that day. He's got good news and bad news, he tells me. First the bad news. We're losing the aide at school. She's being replaced. She's pregnant. I'm relieved. Rio didn't like her much. Neither did I. "I'm sure someone better is on the horizon," I cheerfully add. He hates my attitude. "What's the good news?" I ask. He looks up at me on the staircase. "I was told to tell you that Rio's handwriting is getting better and that it's easier for him now."

Just as I had declared in prayer. Word for word. I asked for a sign. There it was!

Seven weeks in, the psychologist assigned to Rio at school, sits back smiling at Rio's yearly IEP, and makes his report. "Four to six weeks ago," he proudly announces, "Rio made a profound developmental leap out of nowhere."

"What's a leap?" I ask. "Progress," he explains, "is incremental." "A leap, on the other hand, is big. Unexplained." Everyone at the meeting commented on how Rio was changing. I didn't know whether to say anything, but couldn't hold back. I told them I had begun to meditate with him. It got no reaction. Or at best a reaction similar to David's. They were all delighted with the results. He was clearly a different child. But they had no interest in the why. Not if had anything to do with God.

"It's as if," the psychologist concluded, "Rio's Authentic Self has begun to emerge."

And with that I stopped caring whether they heard or agreed. I had nothing to prove. The results were too profound. Rio was getting well. Who cared about the rest?

I left there and immediately went to the beach....to the water... fell to my knees and wept... Overcome by the power of this.

"I can finally say what I'm thinking," I hear Rio tell a beloved aide, Jason, weeks later. And at Christmas, I witness his first real conversation, in his life. About music. With our wonderful neighbor, Maxine. Leave the room and weep. Again.

"All is well in this place"

Indeed.

Unlike David, Jack was thrilled. He wanted every detail.

And with Rio showing so much progress, I offered to do this with the other kids in his special day class. That's code for special Ed. It's supposed to make you feel better, I guess. It doesn't. But now I have a real reason to celebrate. It's working. So, I go to his teacher. I'll come every morning. Surprisingly, he agrees. I write a letter to the parents asking permission. They go for it, assuming it will make them calmer. I'm careful not to bring in God in any way. Not in a public school. Instead, I use the qualities of God. We sit in a circle and I look them and say "I see love everywhere." And they repeat it back to me. "I see Joy." Joy. " Peace." Peace. "Wisdom." Wisdom. "Love." Love. "And if love is everywhere, love is where I am right now." The ones who are verbal repeat what I say, the others I tell to think it. Then, we close our eyes and go into the silence. There were snickers. And squeals. Rocking. And pacing. But for the most part, they sat. I turned to one young girl who was having the hardest time. She hadn't wanted to join the group. She was nonverbal, and spent a considerable part of every-day pacing to and fro, reciting random lines from *Toy*

Story. Reluctantly she had allowed the teacher to lead her to the table. She was trying her best. Grunting. Squirming. I was afraid the other kids would start laughing, so I turned to her and took her hands, knowing I was in the light. We sat that way for a few moments, and when I felt I had pushed her envelope about as far as I could, I let go and began to turn away, and to my great surprise, she reached out for my hands and turned me back. And a week later from the back seat of their car, she initiated her first real sentence.

"I want to sit with Rio's mom," she said.

But she never did again. Her mother, while telling me this news with some excitement, would never allow it again. They never chose to capitalize on that moment. But I've found most people react this way. They don't believe it. It's not science. Even in spite of the evidence. They'd rather attach any reason to this succeeding other than a concept of God. I've spoken to heads of autistic organizations and have gotten a polite show of disinterest. But, the one thing I have also learned is everything is for a reason. Beyond my understanding and judgment. They don't call it a mystery school for nothin'. And I continue to work on her, and others, from a distance.

One of the teachers begins to use meditation in her class, and I go back to a practice of one, Rio. He continues to make progress, in some cases inexplicable. Difficult puzzles that Dr. Bill's team had given up on, are suddenly doable. He's begun to venture out of his special day class to join the general Ed population for English and history, and ultimately, due to the instincts and faith of an exceptional teacher, into honors English. I'm not going to tell you the autism went away, but he was picking up information from everywhere around him. This is unusual for Autistic children. And particularly for Rio. In the past, he had to be taught everything, broken down into small segments, and then hope that it stuck. That he'd remember and generalize the information, apply it appropriately and successfully to other situations. Now suddenly he was using slang. Asking complex questions. Hanging out. Chatting. That summer he attended a summer camp, Day Jams. They were great with him, and he began to compose music. Heavy rock. Metal. With bits of rap thrown in. And develop a genuine fan base. Parents told us they thought he had the makings of a star, even as he jumped and danced awkwardly on the stage. "Our own Joe Cocker," David would say. If only.

I continued to follow the Divine instructions and meditate with him every day. And the following year culminated with his being asked to speak at his middle school commencement, one of six students chosen in a competition that asked the question:

"*What inspires you?*"

And this is what Rio dictated to me, and ultimately read at the ceremony. This boy who had made no sense:

"Inspired for Life" by Rio Wyles

You know, I look out in the world and I see people suffering, sometimes without even water. They're homeless by an earthquake or hurricane or a war. It's nice that we all have a nice place to live, but I think about the people who are living with tragedy. I see them and say, "What if that was me?" "Would I be able to survive?" And that inspires me to want to help.

I feel like I can make a difference. We can all work together to rebuild their homes, even their cities, even their countries, whether it's New Orleans or Iraq. It may cost a lot of money, but we cannot turn our backs on these people and just worry about where our oil is coming from, or buying the latest video game. It's easy to do that. Yep. It's easy to forget them and just think about who's gonna be the next American Idol. Which is cool, too. I'm totally down for Taylor Hicks. He's my man. But, I also care about them.

You know, when I first came here I was nervous. It was new and there was new stuff to learn... challenging stuff. And I thought you weren't going to be so nice. And I thought the teachers were going to be harsh. But I found teachers who were kind and not only accepted me and helped me succeed, but made me feel good about myself. And made me do things I never expected to do. I want to thank these wonderful teachers for appreciating the human being that I am.

Ms. Anger for inviting me into the Honors English class and taking me in a direction I never thought I would go in. And to the kids in honor's English, you're great kids. You made me feel welcome and helped me out. And made me feel like I had something worth listening to. To all of you, I know you'll succeed in your dreams and I know you'll make it far.

Mr. Salazar, for helping find solutions to make the work easier for me, and making me feel respected.

And to Ms. Armstead, for knowing I have hard times, but making me try harder and making me feel I can succeed. And to you other guys in the class, you're noise makers, but your momma jokes were hilarious, and you even laughed at mine and you made me feel like a jokester and that was great.

Ms. Suhr, for appreciating me and giving me the chance to show what I can do. And don't worry so much, Ms. Sur, but I think we'll all turn into intelligent human beings one day.

And Mr. Brumel, for making us run, even though it was painful and you were tough, thank you for believing we could succeed, even when we couldn't. And thank you for making me believe I could do better, and I did.

And finally, Mr. Weggler. You goofball, sometimes you bring out the light. You smile and laugh when I screw up and I appreciated that. You brighten up my day and made me believe I could succeed.

And to all the aides in special Ed, don't lose faith. Keep working hard with these kids. You never know what they *might be able to do. And remember to be kind to them. They're doing their best.*

And to Alicia, thank you for being the great person you are.

And to Joe, for standing with me.

Well, next year I'm off to Hamilton Music Magnet. I'm up to another adventure and I'm ready to succeed at that. For music is what truly inspires me. Music helps us be in harmony with one another. That we look inside ourselves and see that we are here together and that's all that counts.

So lastly, I want to thank my fans. Thank you guys, I appreciate your love and support. You made it the very best school experience that I've ever had.

So here I go. I'm ready to play. Peace y'all.

Was this really my son up there? Saying these words??? Then to add to all this, at some point in the speech, in front of a stadium full of a few thousand people, Rio dropped the paper he was reading from. I sat in my seat, holding my breath. There was a light wind that day and the paper alighted and drifted to the front of the stage. He was nervous and unsure. But he went around the podium, retrieved it and resumed his place, all without missing a beat. It was truly miraculous, how far he'd come. What he was becoming. Emerging into. Revealing. Many, many years later in a trendy sushi spot in Venice, a couple at the next table recognized Rio from that day. The wife told him that the memory of him up there and what he said still makes her cry. I'm not alone. Still does.

And his lyrics for the music he would perform that summer at camp grew increasingly meaningful and memorable. Sometimes heartbreaking. Then, they took a turn and went beyond his immediate circumstance, to something and somewhere else.

You know in life things happen
doesn't seem what it seems
Even in dreams
obstacles may appear.
You may not know when you're here
And time and place and when
It may happen over again.
One day you figure it out.
What your life was all about.
Strange things happening all around you
Looks like karma's come around and it found you.

Do I think it's God? Absolutely. All of it.

Does David? Absolutely not. And loathes the idea of it. It's vile to him. "There is no personal God!" he screams at me.

Once again, I don't care. I'm getting my son back.

I'm walking in a miracle.

Hey Jude.

Chapter 8

By Their Fruits Ye Shall Know Them

Matthew 7:20

"I don't want to be king."

These words slip out. I don't know where they come from. I'm back on my deck, a few weeks after the initial order to meditate with him. The progress Rio's making is so startling, I suddenly fear that it's going to catapult us into some kind of limelight. And for some reason this odd choice of words, "I don't want to be king", comes out. And equally startling, I hear a voice answer clearly:

"There will be no king.
You will each have your own at-one-ment with God."

When? Where? What world will this be in?

"You're the only one who didn't want to be king then.
And you're the only one now."

And for some reason, I think of Jonathan.

I dream I'm in New York somewhere on Eighth or Ninth Avenue, in front of a greengrocer, camped out, seated on a crate, surrounded by bins of fruit and vegetables and flowers, waiting for my father and son who've left me here.

They're coming back.

To get me.

Chapter 9

For Everything

a season

and a reason

Jack begins to dream. The first one right out of the Bible. A tree has been cut down that is growing in his head. Only the stump survives, surrounded by weeds.

Somehow, I know this dream, it feels oddly familiar, and that it's biblical. I've never read the Book of Daniel, where I ultimately find it. Yet somehow, I know its meaning; the language of dreams suddenly second nature. In the dream, the tree, the consciousness of God, has been severed, and is surrounded by weeds. The garden, all that surrounds the tree, untended, ignored. And once again our relationship changes. Still Jonathan and Saul, but as more dreams come, it's as if two new characters and their story have come alive in us... as us. Informing the dreams, but more than that, defining, crafting our relationship, and once again, our relationship brings life and deeper meaning to the biblical story.

This time, of a great king, of the kingdom of Babylon. Who refuses to forsake his own will and a desire to be worshiped, to a greater God. And a young man, Daniel, who he takes captive. A boy who the King came to trust, love, and honor, but in a flash, could just as easily annihilate. And as to the boy, you can almost feel his concern, if not love for this King, as he interprets his dreams, and sees the danger looming. As he tries to warn Nebuchadnezzar of his faltering relationship with God. As I had with Jack that day. "You've lost your connection to God." This King who holds him prisoner. It feels all too familiar.

More and more I feel that I am there against my will, prisoner, captive. A power that drives me there, holds me there, that's far from working in my best interest. There are days when it's pouring rain, and I run to meet him at eight a.m. to get my fix. And there he is, drenched, waiting. Yes, there's love, and like Daniel, I'm hoping he'll find his way to higher ground. But more and more this love is tinged with addiction. But equally true, I'm growing more and more steeped in God as these stories come alive in us. I feel like Daniel, and Daniel feels like me. And Jack, so much like this King.

And as I begin to read this biblical story, in light of my own, I'm struck that Daniel was given the Chaldean name of Belteshazzar – "the woman who protects the King", one translation offers. And I wonder where Daniel really was, when in a fit of rage Nebuchadnezzar, this king, ordered Daniel's three compatriots to their death in a fiery furnace, for refusing to bow to him. Who was this king of this world who wanted to be worshiped? And who was this boy he brought from Jerusalem into bondage who refused to dine at his -- the King's -- table? Found his food, what he was taking in, unclean? I never bought that Daniel was out of town when his friends faced that gruesome dance with death, which is the explanation that is given by most scholars. Or if he was, that it was by chance. For I knew in my heart, that Nebuchadnezzar could no more have killed Daniel, than Jack could kill me. Because he loved him. But I also couldn't divorce this image of death and a fiery furnace from those that would follow at Auschwitz and Birkenau, Sobibor, Treblinka. That somehow all of this was connected. And that I was being called... away from this....away from him... into the wilderness....to God. And every part of my life was orchestrating to get me there, including him.

"You're not supposed to be here."

Jack dreams again. He repeats the warning that's been given while he sleeps, only this time, as he tells it, he looks me straight in the eye:

"You're not supposed to be here."

In the dream, he's on a newly paved road, men in white space suits finishing the job, smoothing the concrete, the galaxy as a backdrop. Beautiful. Very sci-fi. But, he's cheated his way in through a side entrance, not the main gate, and he's been caught. A man in a white pickup stops him and issues the warning.

"You're not supposed to be here."
Jack agrees.
"What do you think," asks the man?
"Pretty cool," Jack replies.

Jack looks deep into my eyes, passing on the man's warning, as the man in the dream repeats it for good measure, along with instructions:

"You're not supposed to be here.
There's a freeway on your left.
Be careful when you merge into traffic."

The next day I'm due at the studio for a table reading of one of my scripts. The 405 is Jammed. It's Friday afternoon and I'm getting nowhere. On top of that, emergency vehicles race to an accident up ahead. I pull off and try the access road. Even worse. I swerve into the left-hand lane to get back on the freeway, when suddenly I find myself careening into the back of a truck at forty miles an hour, with no idea of how I got there. Like time was lost. The truck pulls over. The front of my car is an accordion, creamed. He says I caught him by surprise, surveys the damage to his vehicle, and concludes that he can't blame me for any of it. Can't say it was my fault. It was a clear rear-ender, open and shut. Now I'm the one caught by surprise. None of this makes sense. I embrace him and thank him, relieved as he drives away.

The next day the insurance company takes care of everything, even my rates stay the same. I come out smelling like a rose. In a rental car, I'm back on the freeway driving to my shrink in the valley, thinking about the accident. What could it possibly mean? Suddenly Jack's dream pops into my mind and the warning: "You're not supposed to be here. There's a freeway on your left. ... Be careful..."

My shrink suggests I let the universe know I got the message. They can tone it down. They obviously mean business. You're not supposed to be here.

I don't know what came first, my beginning to leave, or his flirting with the idea of another woman. Can it get any worse? I thought we already hit bottom with the first betrayal. Wrong again. Humiliation awaits. The wilderness is looking better every day. And everything in life seems ever more determined to get me there, beginning and ending with this. I begin to slip away, just in time, as the new woman appears. She's all over him. Only unlike Cuba, this time I get to watch. That beautiful place of mine, with its floor to ceiling windows, becomes my front row seat, as he chooses to carry on this seduction directly in front of me by the water's edge. "I hurt people," he'd warned. You got that right. It makes me sick. Breaks my heart. How could he do this to me? Hurt me this way? Be so cruel? I discover all this one morning when I failed to have a proper breakfast for Rio before school. And as I was running to Starbucks to grab him a muffin, I heard a voice deep within admonish me, 'You're not feeding your son." I knew it was right, in both cases. I was neither placing any Divine Son, nor Rio first in the food chain. It was way too much about Jack, or pulling away from Jack, or dating other men to forget Jack, or missing Jack. It was true. I was not feeding my son. So, it was not surprising that morning of the message and the muffin, and getting him to school late, that I also returned to find someone parked in my space at the apartment. The Universe was clearly not working in my favor. I was out of alignment. And as I climbed those same stairs I had found so charming that night in the fog, I turned just in time before I headed into the apartment, to catch a glimpse of him on the beach, with her. Whoever she was. I watched as she flirts and flits about him, throwing Max the Frisbee. Jogging with him. Taking my place.

I don't need to see more. I'm gone.

I run into his friend from the cafe a few weeks later. He's sullen. He says her name, his voice dripping with disdain. He's not a fan. I know it's said out of love for me, and I love him for it. I stop by the restaurant when the coast is clear, and all the staff asks me where I've been. They miss me. And I miss them. I try not to watch every morning. The pain of this betrayal is overwhelming. I want the feeling, all my feelings, to go away just like they did with Frank, when I met the other woman. They all vanished. Shut off. But unlike that experience, this time seeing the two of them only intensifies the pain. I accidentally walk in on them one morning. She's playing with his feet. I want to vomit.

In a guided meditation, in a class I'm taking in the midst of all this, I'm asked to imagine my relationship with God. And I see myself, so clearly from behind, hanging suspended in the air directly in front of the sun, sporting a pair of white wings, spread open wide. Not so much angel. More bird. The wings of a great, white bird.

I run into Jack at a party. He comes over, excited to see me, anxious to talk. But this time, it's me who's cold. "You've lost the privilege of my presence," I manage to get out. Not bad. I like how that sounds. The privilege of my presence. Appropriately self-respecting. Something that's been sorely lacking.

"I'll get rid of her. She means nothing," he offers.

He says this to make me feel better. And it does.

"Then why did you do it?" I never ask. Is this the way you feel? Do you hurt us so we can feel the way you do? Or are you really this callous and cruel?

Or is his act with her simply trying to get me where I refuse to go willingly? "You're not supposed to be here." I hate the idea, resent it, that I'm being asked to give it all up. To give him up. For what? The love of God? This new kind of love? I'm still not ready for it. Just a silly woman in love, who's been hurt. And who's won...for the moment. "I'll get rid of her." That's all he had to say and the pain is gone. Forget God. Forget the warnings. Forget seeking kingdoms. Even love thy neighbor. She didn't care about me. Why should I care about her? It's small, and I feel small thinking it. But I'm too happy at the moment. Yes, get rid of her. Without actually saying the words, he knows what he has to do.

And does the next day. Purely by chance, I pass by the window as she tries to grab him, to kiss him, and he literally runs from her, like some ten-year-old. She comes to me, days later, devastated. I offer some stupid consoling words, but want to say, "Who did you think I was? What did you think I was doing here? Was it so easy to buy his line that I was just a friend? Or did it never come up?" Any woman knows exactly what's going on when she comes on the scene. We're equipped with that kind of radar. Unless you don't want to know. When I first met Jack, I would always defer to his ex-wife. When she'd appear, I'd disappear. Like some polygamous pecking order. Until the day he told me to stay, not to leave. She was the one who left. But this new girl had no interest in me, even now as she came to me for solace and answers, with a broken heart.

I tell him about her visit and her emotional state, when he returns home the following week, having conveniently cut out of town -- coward. The news is met on his part with a cold silence, and I begin to wonder if he has a heart. Sometimes, I get this feeling that he's lost in there....buried. It's in his work. Bars over metal windows that slide up and down, revealing glimpses of beauty just beyond. A prisoner. Maybe he really was abducted by aliens that day when he was seven. And they took his heart. And his soul. "You in there?" I'd sometimes call to him....deep within.

Gloomy Sunday

I'd recently read a myth I thought he might be living. Not biblical this time, but Norse, in which Odin loses his eye. And wondered if Jack would lose his eye?

"Horrible thought."

"Cancel that," I added quickly, warding off any danger as I head into the movie and take my seat. I'm here on my

mother's recommendation. A foreign film called "Gloomy Sunday". It's the story of a Jewish man, Szabo, who's living with a sultry Hungarian girl, above the restaurant he owns. And while she does nothing for me, it's clear, based on the reaction of all the men, and a kind of steamy bathtub moment, that she's meant to be a femme fatale. I personally think she's crazy. Szabo's a great guy... cool, elegant, sexy, in that French leading man kind of way. But Ileana's drawn in two other hopefuls, both of whom attempt suicide as she strings them along. Takes them as lovers? Hard to tell. But they both want it all, irresistibly drawn to her. She's like a siren in Odysseus, calling them in, watching them crash. The first succeeds and takes his life, a composer, who plays piano in Szabo's place and writes the title's gloomy song. The other, a young German, heads to a bridge but is stopped by Szabo just as he's about to jump. He's got his whole life in front of him, Szabo tells him. Don't end it over this. It's not worth it. She's not worth it. Hans listens and takes the risk that life will offer him something this alluring again.

What it does offer is revealed some years later, when Hans returns, this time as a member of the SS, on a mission to round up the Jews and either kill them, or ship them off to death camps. He assures Szabo that in return for saving a young, foolish boy years back, that he will save Szabo now. No matter what's going on around him, not to worry. And Hans makes good on his word, as Szabo's Jewish neighbors are rounded up and shot, in the country-side over mass graves, or in the Town Square. It's all over very quickly. Szabo survives, the last Jew, married now to his shiksa heartbreaker of a girlfriend. He's safe.

Till one night, when Hans shows up at the restaurant with a comrade, a Nazi chum. They've been drinking and Hans is different. Something's changed and Szabo knows it.

"Tell me a joke," Hans orders his old friend, in menacing good humor.
"Tell me a Jewish joke. I like Jewish jokes."

It's clear Szabo's life is on the line.
Szabo begins.
"There's a commandant named Mueller with one glass eye."

The eye is a masterpiece. So real, he likes to play a game with the Prisoners arriving at the camp. He brings the Jews before him, one by one, gun pointed in their faces, and asks the simple question:

"Which one's the glass eye?"

If they guess right, they live.
If not, they're shot on the spot.
The first victim is yanked forward, gun trained.
"Which one's the glass eye?" Mueller barks.

"The left one sir," the Jew responds, hurried, but confident.

Mueller's surprised. Maybe the fake's not as good as he thought.

"How did you know so quickly?" he asks.

A beat, and the Jew delivers a deliberate and dangerous response.

"It's the only one that has any feeling for me."

It's one of those classic movie moments where all the diners in the restaurant are silent, riveted, terrified, understanding all the implications of the joke, and the power Hans wields over Szabo's life at this moment, maybe even their own. They breathlessly await his fate. The tension breaks as Hans suddenly laughs at this dark bit of humor, as does his chum, then the others in the restaurant, and in the theatre around me. Relief. Knowing Szabo is safe. Enjoying the joke. But there I am in the midst of it, tears in my eyes. For all the Jews who died in that atrocious moment in history. And because I had just asked the question, would Jack lose his eye?

And his last name is Mueller.

There's a commandant named Mueller with one glass eye.

Who is this guy?

Some months later he dreams about his mother, who's at the heart of his broken heart. In the dream, she's dressed in a striped uniform behind barbed wire. And on the other side of the fence, are the people in charge, or perhaps just everyday folk who stood by and did nothing -- His father, the rest of his siblings, and him. I gasp as he tells me the dream. He looks at me and covers one eye.

You're not supposed to be here.

"I gave up a great love once out of obligation, I won't do it again."

My own words to Jesus in a dream echo.

He's come to stay with me, along with Mary. But, in the dream I'm meeting Jack at the café. We haven't seen each other for a while, and we long to, and arrange to meet for lunch. I could take Jesus with me, but it will ruin everything, change everything.

"I gave up a great love once in my life out of obligation," I tell him, "and I won't do it again."

I leave and run to the cafe and there's Jack waiting, where I always find him, and we fall into a deep passionate kiss, as if there was no end to this love. The restaurant's empty, all ours, and inside he's cleared away the tables and chairs, off to the sides. And as the light falls, the room is warmed by the glow of small, white, twinkling Christmas lights that line the wall behind him. In the center of the room, he leans back in a chair, holding out his hand to mine, as I circle him, to that great Frank Loesser's classic, "Baby, It's Cold Outside"

"I really can't stay...

But baby it's cold outside

I've got to go away...

Chapter 10

The Mother of All Puzzle Pieces

I begin to notice, that when I see Jack, the healing of Rio stops. And when I leave him, it picks up again. Blossoms. Almost all our contact is when Rio's at school, so it has nothing to do with any interaction between them, or even knowledge on Rio's part that I see him. No, I feel like I'm being given a choice. The warnings, the dreams, the accident, the heartache, the humiliation, none of it has worked. So God's laying it on the line. It's Jack or Rio. You can't have both.

And where I would have died for Jack, and the attraction and hold is still incredibly strong, crazy as that sounds…. there is no choice. There never was, or ever would be. This is my son. Rio. My sweetness. My heart. The nicest guy in the whole world. A chance for him to interact, to speak to people. To heal. To experience, if not a normal life, something close to it, or closer to it. Any Autistic person will tell you of the loneliness and isolation they feel that is devastating. Neglected and ignored, notwithstanding their creativity and kindness, and so often a fierce intelligence and wisdom often missing in the "normal" peers who reject them. No, there is no choice. I have to go, and begin to leave, more and more, without saying anything. Just slowly disappearing. No formal ending or proclamation, likely because I don't trust myself to follow through. There've been so many goodbyes that didn't last. But the stakes this time are impossibly high. Nice work, God.

But like any addict, one day at a time.

For weeks, I see him outside the window every morning and force myself to turn away. This last temptation. Someone suggests I cut the invisible cords that bind us, and in meditation, I do just that. I have to forget him. Finally, I draw the curtains, shutting out the world. Then thankfully, at some point, I notice he's not there. He's gone. Likely back to Cuba, or the Ranch. The later, I find out. For ten whole days the beach is mine....all mine. No seeing him. A time to wean myself. The curtains fly open. It's a relief. I'm determined to use this time to let go. Really let go.

A few days in, eyes closed in meditation, I feel a fine spray on my face. I open my eyes to find Max standing there, nose to nose with me. Shaking the water off his coat. Happy. Tail wagging. And Jack, a few feet away, hanging back.

"Did you tell him to come over?" I ask, suspicious, amused and flattered ...still. And happy....still. Damn.

"No, I tried to keep him away. I knew you were in meditation. But a wave brought him right to you." A wave? God?

He continued on with his run, and I closed my eyes, back into the silence. But distracted, again. Conflicted, but smiling. I couldn't leave the beach without saying hello. I'd never said goodbye. Just left. That would be the end. A definite end. Door shut. For good. Cold and unfeeling. That wasn't us. Not after all this time. I couldn't do it. I'll just say hello, join him for the final tosses of the Frisbee to Max in the water, and be gone.

Yeah, like just one chip.

The next thing I know we're back at the café, washing my feet, laughing, having coffee and planning the next day and the day after that. And happy. People move in and out of our conversation, as that thread silently weaves us together, once again. The rest of the day I walk in that magic. Some separation. A whole two weeks. But maybe I'm only imagining Rio's ups and downs, I thought. Maybe it's all in my mind. Maybe I don't have to choose. Maybe God brought that wave. Maybe I can have it all! Maybe this whole thing is bloody nuts!! Maybe I am!

Later that day, David drops Rio off, having picked him up from a therapy he was suddenly excelling at. "How did it go?" I asked joyfully, expectantly, wanting more and more happy news to heap upon my glow, in my beautiful castle by the water, Jack back in my life.

"Terribly," David answered. "It's like the autism's back."

Everything stopped. Like a cold wind blowing through.

All right, that's it. I don't know who this cat is, but he is out of my life. I apologized to Rio that night -- It can't be fun, the ups and downs -- and committed myself to the work we were doing together. I was convinced now more than ever, that Rio and I were in this together. That we came here to do this work -- meditating, healing, autism --all of it -- partners in crime in this increasingly wondrous adventure.

"I gave you the child," is what I heard that night. Indeed, he did. Together, thick and thin.

And the more I walked in God, the more I knew that at my death I'd regret not taking this journey full out, to fully see where it's trying to lead. That the most I'd be is the girl who almost made it. That I had to leave Jack. That it was over. Finito. Basta. Done. So, the next morning, before we went into meditation I reiterated my promise, my pledge, my commitment, to myself and to my son, and Rio looked at me and began to sing:

*"She's not just a pretty face.
She's got everything it takes.
She's the mother of the human race."*

"Rio....," I asked incredulously, "what are you singing?"

"It's Shania Twain, Mommy."

I was speechless. Remembering the dream from nine years before. Of the man with the gun who wanted to meet Shania Twain. Only now did the symbolism become perfectly clear. The mother of the human race. Eve. I may have emitted an audible gasp, then told him the dream. And, as I recounted it, for the first and only time, I saw the image from the dream of 2049 Century Park East imploding from the top, and realized it was the same picture I would see on TV six years later. The World Trade Center. The Twin Towers.

For you see, 2049 has a twin, 2029, and is a twin, I come to discover that day, designed by the same man who created those architectural feats – those tallest buildings -- the Towers destroyed in New York on 9/11.

The mother of the human race. Eve.

And the man with a gun who's come to meet her.

Presumably to kill her.

In the Twin Towers.

I said my goodbyes – a real goodbye -- that morning, after Rio left for school, filling Jack in on this most recent, stunning revelation. The final one we'd share for a very long time. His friend joined us at the end, and remarked how full of enthusiasm I was. And I thought of a reading -- a quote of Albert Schweitzer's from his *Philosophy of Civilization* -- that had spoken to me, in which Schweitzer said, that "nothing of real value in this world is ever accomplished without self-sacrifice and enthusiasm," the later term literally meaning God possessed. The former, 'sacrifice', translating to nothing more than making room for the sacred. Room to be filled with something greater. I had thought of sharing that quote of Schweitzer's with Jack earlier that day, and its meaning in all this, but decided against it. Too heavy, I thought. Shania in the Towers was enough. And here was God showing up to underscore its significance in my life.

"She's not just a pretty face," Jack added as I walked away.

And, as I stepped back onto the beach, into my wilderness, I was filled with awe and that feeling of magic, the one that met me on the beach that first day. And I felt free. The string that had tied my heart to his was joining me on my journey. Swirling around me, in me. And I left behind any resentment I had carried for so long for being asked to give up this love. This sacrifice that God seemed to be requiring. For if sacrifice meant nothing more than making room for the sacred, I knew I needed all I could get. For with the appearance of Shania and the World Trade Center, I suddenly had the feeling that the story that was unfolding in my life was bigger and went beyond any personal heartache or happiness. That I was tapping into the story of the collective. The group. The world story. And that somehow that story-- the myth of this tallest building Campbell had alluded to - the Towers - coming down, is somehow connected to a story from very long ago. Right back to Eve, the Mother of the human race. The Beginning.

And the feeling that somehow the sacrifice of Jack for God has meaning in all this.

That my giving him up has meaning.

That my choosing God over him, has meaning.

3

The

Myth

Chapter 11

In The Beginning

Eve. The mother of the human race. And a guy who wants to meet her...presumably to kill her. What went on in the garden? What happened there? And what could it possibly have to do with the Towers?

I'm guessing, my knowledge of this particular story is on par with most. Adam and Eve in a garden, eat fruit from a tree that was off limits. They'd been warned by God not to eat of this tree, this forbidden fruit. But a snake convinced the woman it was all hogwash. Take a bite of the apple...what's to hurt? And it was downhill from there. No more cush life. No garden. Not for them, or any other human being. They were tossed out to fend for themselves. Adam, to make his way by the "sweat of his brow." Eve, to suffer in childbirth. And the snake? Well, he continued to eat the dust.

But on closer examination, I see there's a whole lot more to this story. And my dream begins to become clear. This time I go straight to the source: Genesis. So, what exactly did go on?

There was this tree in the center of the garden, just beside the tree of life. The tree of knowledge of good and evil. God instructed Adam that he could eat of any tree, but that one, warning him that to eat of its fruit will surely bring death. It's at that point, I learn, that God creates the woman for Adam, sensing his loneliness. Presumably Adam told the woman the skinny on the tree, but may have embellished it, or else we're witnessing the first round of whispering down the lane, for when the serpent asks Eve if God had warned against eating from this tree, she adds, "...or even touch it, for we will die."[9] I could almost hear the serpent laughing when he responds, with a voice reminiscent of George Sanders in *Jungle Book*: "To the contrary, 'you won't die'[10]...rather 'You'll be like God'[11]."Then the book says, Eve took one look at the fruit, saw that it was good to eat, and took a bite. Then shared it with her husband. And all hell broke loose, lots of finger pointing, as God speaks to each of them.

The first thing I find surprising and odd, is that God doesn't speak to Adam and Eve in the garden on that fateful day way back when. No, he speaks to the Serpent and Eve. And then to Adam, separately. I find that so interesting. Like Adam's some kinda' third wheel. I know, I know, one could say that Eve and the Serpent were more culpable, but it's what God says to them that peaks my interest. And, considering his complete and immediate forgiveness of Eve that is highly attractive, I'm of the mind that Adam's deserving of more than odd man out. But odd man out, he is. And admittedly it's the kind of forgiveness that if you're in

---

[9] Genesis 3:3
[10] Genesis 3:4
[11] Genesis 3:5

love with someone else, it's not all that welcome, and can be downright oppressive, even suffocating. I mean, imagine the Hollywood version. The long-suffering cuckolded husband willing to forgive. To take her back, despite her transgression. It's the kind of love that becomes a poison, a prison, if she longs for someone else. Rhett's love was a prison to Scarlett – discovering her mistake way too late. We loved it when Rhett finally told her to shove it with this Ashley thing. Or Bette Davis in Somerset Maugham's *The Letter*. Which was worse? Her lover Geoff, cruelly tossing her off for a native woman (a story that's startling close for comfort, sans the murder), or her husband willing to forgive her, stay with her, stand by her, even buying the infamous letter, paying the blackmail that could land her on death row? Yet even after all these good acts, his love was an anathema to her. She longed for Geoff, only Geoff, the lover she had killed, after being so cruelly rejected by him.

Or Victor Lazlo. We admired him, but felt what his love was doing to Ilsa, in light of her feelings for Rick, her true love. Did we believe she would finally forget Rick and come to love Victor? I came over time in this journey to hope so. To hope she fell in love with him, and his nobility, and didn't spend the rest of her days longing for Rick.

But why deal with the serpent in these terms, like a leading man? I mean we're talking your basic *Serpens Vipera*. Or are we? "From this day," God proclaims to the snake, "you will crawl, dine on the dust."[12] Wait a minute, he was a standing dude? "And I will put enmity between you and the woman." [13] Didn't they hate each other already?

---

[12] Genesis 3:14
[13] Genesis 3:15

I'm mean, he had just led her down some garden path, and now there they were, just the two of them, the snake and the woman, standing before the judgment of the Almighty, surely ample cause for hate. Apparently, not. God made sure there was to be enmity between them. Insisted on it. Declared it. Demanded it! That got me thinking that a lot more was at play here than mere disobedience over a piece of fruit.

And then God adds the kicker, as he says to Eve, or rather commands: "And your desire *shall be* to thy husband."[14] That emphasis is not mine. It's in the book!

Why is God telling her that? I always assumed the snake was a snake and she ate an apple. And frankly, I could never really understand what all the fuss was about. And now, God declares they're to be enemies. And her desire shall be towards her husband. As opposed to who? The snake???

Who is this guy? Who offers Eve the opportunity to be a like a god. [15]

> *How art thou fallen from heaven, O Lucifer, son of the morning,*
> *bright morning star,*
> *Whose desire was to set his throne above the stars of God.*
>
> **Isaiah 14.**

---

[14] Genesis 3:16
[15] Genesis 3:5

Lucifer? That great looking angel, who, according to this, desired to sit above God?

model of perfection, full of wisdom and perfect in beauty.
in Eden, adorned with every precious stone, as a guardian cherub.

Ezekiel 28:11-19

He was there?! In Eden? Adorned with jewels?! As a guardian angel?!! I never understood the allure of what he offered her, to be greater than God. And now that I'm into the story, don't buy it as an enticement for Eve. It's not in her nature. Not someone as unformed and submissive as Eve. I mean she's only been around for what? A few weeks? But, according to Isaiah, it is his. This was his desire he was articulating – to set his throne above God -- an extraordinary display of narcissism, perhaps the first on the planet. And, true to that nature, just assumed it was the desire of everyone, or should be. But she went for it, this offer, I believe for a whole other reason.

Replace the snake in Genesis seducing the woman with a great looking angel, and it starts to make sense, and becomes an entirely different kind of story. And the tree was pleasing to her eyes and the food was good,[16] as much as she knew it was forbidden. For the fruit that she consumed, I believe, was him. And the act was sexual, passionate, even

---

[16] Genesis 3:6

love, at least for her. I think Eve fell in love with him. And, ultimately, he couldn't resist her.

Once again, my own relationship with Jack floods my consciousness, vibrating, resonating with this story, informing it. The seduction, wanting me there, but fighting it. My falling in love. His inability to finally resist. How explosive the passion was that night. How guilty he felt after. He said he felt he had betrayed her. I think there's truth to that... who she is in this story... who I am in this story. But the feeling of betrayal he experienced, I believe, went back to this story, and God.

Or maybe I'm just being a silly romantic and Lucifer's just cruel. That there's nothing nice about him. That he never loved her. That his only intention was to destroy her, and the man, right from the git-go, born of his jealousy of these humans who had captured God's attention and heart. No longer being numero uno. After all, until they came along he'd held that favored position. But if he was only fueled by hatred, why would God find the need to put enmity between him and the woman? And command Eve that her desire was to be for her husband?

And if there's one thing I've come to know for sure, there are no whoops moments in God. Lucifer was neither a surprise nor a mistake. Like everything else in this book, he had a purpose. The Clergy, I'm finding, uniformly say God was testing her. Her obedience to him. After all, he had forbidden Eve and Adam to eat of this fruit. Like a child, they preach, once you tell them not to touch something, it's irresistible. To want what you can't have. I think there's great truth in that statement, but it's not, I believe, what happened here. Yes, it was an act of defiance, but the motivation was not the act of a willful child who must be brought into submission. To the contrary, I believe it was love. All around.

God wanted Eve, this woman he created, for himself. For the man made in his image. But he wanted her to want him, consciously. To choose him, consciously. Willingly. Desire him. Not like some robot or automaton. Or out of obligation. Lucifer was not an accident. Or a surprise. He was a plant. An essential part of the story. Falling into form – into the duality of good and evil -- was the only way. Having the right to choose. To find her way back. To him. To God.

But for now, Eve was forced to leave the garden, and her lover. And go off with a man she was told she must desire. I wondered how she felt. What their relationship was like? What their marriage was all about? Was there love?

And as God had warned, the moment their passion was consummated, that Eve tasted of this fruit, death entered the story, and these once eternal beings began to die.

But I saw another kind of death in the enmity that was placed between the woman and this dark angel, between her seed and his, that would play out over time as wars, pogroms, crucifixions, inquisitions, annihilation, extermination and genocide.

And, finally, death in the form of a child born from this unholy union.

The first murderer.

> *The kingdom of heaven is like unto leaven which a woman took, and hid in three measures of meal, till the whole was leavened.*
>
> *Matthew 13:33*

Death itself.

A son named Cain.

Chapter 12
The Mystery
Revealed

"Are you telling me that Cain is the son of Lucifer and Eve???" I'm sitting on the beach in meditation when I ask this question. "That what happened in the Garden was a sexual act -- this bite of the apple -- that resulted in a son named Cain? The murderer? I mean, I'm no scholar of the Bible, but that's not exactly conventional wisdom, let alone in the biblical account, I come to find. But this thought has nagged at me ever since I read the story. I want to be damn sure. So, I ask.

When I opened my eyes, a stranger appeared, oddly dressed in Lederhosen. Now mind you, this is the same beach of my awakening, and the same beach of the magic troll, so anything's possible. This time it's a guy in hot pants with suspenders who approaches and immediately asks:

"Where's your dog?"

"I don't have a dog," I answered.

"Oh, you know... that dog you're always with."

I'd never seen this man before, and never did again.

"Oh, that dog," referring to Max. *"I love that dog. And that dog loves me. He's my friend's dog."*

"Where's your friend," the man inquired?

"Away," I responded, keeping it short.

At which point he held out his hand and made a proper introduction:

"Brother Cain," was all he said.

And just to make sure the answer to my question came through perfectly clear, the following day at a Hollywood party, as I was sharing this story with a new friend, a Christian, the only person there who'd be vaguely interested in all this, the production designer from the show leaned in and inquired:

"Hey Judith, how do you like that Cain Cabernet you're drinking?"

We both looked down at the label in disbelief.

An isolated scholar or two, I later learn, have put forth this idea that Cain was the result of an illicit affair between the snake and Eve, as opposed to Adam and Eve, as universally thought, and taught. And while not directly stated, as I begin to read this story, I see that it's actually inferred in scripture. Beginning in Genesis, Cain is not listed among the descendants of Adam. Interesting. Nor is Abel for that matter, which of course gets me thinking. Only Seth.[17]

And even more telling, a handful of words I come across in 1 John 3:12:

---

[17] Genesis 5:1-3

> "Cain, who was of that wicked one."

But I believe this is truth most of all, because it is what God, not so subtly, seemed to be telling me. Cain was not influenced by, but literally of him. John was right. Which led me to the obvious conclusion, in no uncertain terms, that the act in the garden, the fall, was sexual.

This notion of what happened in the Garden is also, I come to discover, reinforced by a small, obtuse story a little later with Noah -- of Ham's coming across his father, drunk, unconscious, naked and uncovered. Uncovered, being the operative word here.

> *And he drank of the wine, (Noah, that is) and was drunken; and he was uncovered within his tent.*
> *And Ham, the father of Canaan, saw the nakedness of his father, and told his two brethren without.*
>
> **Genesis 9:21-22**

Ham runs to tell his brothers, who immediately approach their father with their backs to him and cover him.

> *And Shem and Japheth took a garment, and laid [it] upon both their shoulders, and went backward, and covered the nakedness of their father; and their faces [were] backward, and they saw not their father's nakedness.*

Genesis 9:23

Ham, as a result of this act of discovery, and seeming gossip, even derision, is cursed by his father, Noah.

And Noah awoke from his wine, and knew what his younger son had done unto him.
And he said, Cursed [be] Canaan;
a servant of servants shall he be unto his brethren.

Genesis 9:24-25

Or more exactly, the curse is put on his son, Canaan, for the father's sin. Make that unborn son, Canaan, I discover. How close that is to Cain. Two men in the Bible whose sons are cursed. One arising from the garden. One in this story. But in Noah's case, what could all of this mean? A curse? Over a little embarrassment? I mean, the guy passed out drunk. Naked. He bears some responsibility.

This story has boggled the minds of scholars and once again, I find, is taught primarily as a morality tale of respect for one's elders, or the perils of drink, or to look past one another's faults.

But was there more to this crime that deserved such a punishment? Of seeing his father uncovered? I had a feeling it carried a deeper meaning, and a quick Google revealed it most certainly did.

And the man that lieth with his father's wife

hath uncovered his father's nakedness

Leviticus 20:11.

Read in the context of Leviticus, it's pretty clear what went on. Ham, the son of Noah, slept with his father's wife, while Noah, her husband, lay unconscious/drunk. He slept with his bloody mother! While his father was passed out drunk. And, as a result, an unborn child named Canaan is cursed. Now, think about that symbolically, in connection with the Garden. For I believe this later story exists to clarify what went on there, of a son who slept with the "mother", resulting in a child that is cursed, named Canaan(Cain).

Three characters. Same story. Adam, Eve and Lucifer. Noah, his wife, and Ham.

And I find it so interesting when I learn that the line of Ham, this very son, gives rise to the great empire Babylon and its king, Nebuchadnezzar, who will destroy Israel and take her captive. Including Daniel. Once again, straight out of the garden and the enmity God declared between the woman and the snake.

And then, it hit me. Like some great third act twist. Is that what these stories are about? From the Old to the New? These three characters? The Garden story, over, and over! Adam, Eve and Lucifer!!

It suddenly all makes sense. Why Jonathan drifted between Saul and David, inextricably tied to the dark (his father), but drawn to the light (albeit in David, a flawed light). The relationship between David and Jonathan was like that of a man and a woman (2 Samuel 1:26) because it is! It's Adam and Eve!

Saul's jealousy of David. His absolute hatred of him. Wanting to annihilate him. It's certainly not earned in this later story. Yes, Saul was upset over losing the throne. But his darkness. His melancholy. His relentless pursuit of David, regardless of the fact that David is willing to let him play out his term. The rage. It wasn't about this story. It's about who Saul is! Lucifer. And who David really is! Adam. And who Jonathan is! Eve. It carries the energy of the story from the beginning because that's who they are!

As this truth floods my consciousness, I suddenly see the Yellow Star of David sewn on their coats, their school clothes. Jude. Jew. As he killed "David" over and over. A deep grief rises in me as tears come, as I realize its relationship, in horror. It's all the same energy. It's all an ongoing story dating back to the Garden. If anyone's ever contemplated the enduring nature of Anti-Semitism, that rises time and again, like some Energizer bunny that just won't quit – look no further. It's this story. This relationship. Literally, its Genesis. It's them. It's us. We're living it! We're playing out their story!

I'm hooked. Moving from story to story, character to character. I feel like Patty Duke in that extraordinary scene in *The Miracle Worker* that still makes me cry as I write this, where she understands for the first time at the well, that these letters Annie Sullivan has been spelling out in her hand, these words, have meaning. Running from object to object. Water! Tree! Ground! Mother! Yes!!

It suddenly all makes sense. How hard God was on Saul. How little patience he had for him. I mean compared to David, Saul's transgressions seem minor, to say the least. But knowing who he really is, the selection of Saul now reveals an undiscovered depth. "You want a king?" "Someone other than me?" he seems to be saying, "Here, take him!" Great looking guy... heads above the rest... a real standout. But don't be fooled. The guy's got "baggage".[18]

Knowing who Saul is also makes his refusal to kill Agag – his defying of God's order -- redolent with meaning. Agag, the Amalekite -- who lives only to destroy Israel – the old and the infirm running from bondage. The children who have fallen behind, separated from their parents. Picked off one by one. Agag and his people are evil itself. His refusal to kill their king – a king of this world, like himself – represented Lucifer/Saul's identification with evil, his attachment to it. And most of all his refusal to eliminate it. That is what cost him God's favor, as the Spirit departed from him and cast him into a very lonely and painful darkness. Madness itself. He made his choice.

And it is this very same evil that he refused to eliminate when given the chance, I discover, that rises again in the story of Esther. What do you know, it's all connected. And what Saul/Lucifer failed to do - Sacrifice evil --Eliminate it -- will now fall upon the Woman, Esther. An evil who looks so good at first. Who she falls in love with....again. Wow!

---

[18] 1 Samuel 10:22 When the people come to first meet their new king, he is found hidden amongst the baggage. Not only is he fleeing from his calling – the anointing on his life – I think it's a rather savvy clue. The guy's got baggage. Amazing how current the Bible really is – how many so called modern concepts and expressions have their beginning in these pages. How cool is God? Very cool.

In every Hero's Journey, there comes a point when the hero must return from the magical land into which he or she has crossed, back to home. But carrying a reward. A prize, earned. A magical elixir. Or grail. Or, simply an understanding that has the power to heal. I believe what follows from this point on, is mine.

You ready? Here goes. My moment at the well. Your E-ticket ride. You don't need to have read the Bible to understand what follows. I've given you all you need. But don't let me stop you. And don't let it stop you. It will all make sense. And more importantly, it holds the key to our individual lives, to the mythic tale unfolding in us, and around us, right now.

Grab your popcorn and buckle up. Here we go.

Esther.[19] In Hebrew, "The Megillah", means "the hidden", conjuring up for me the image of the Garden, once again, when they hid from God, now aware and ashamed of their nakedness. Most scholars would say what is hidden in the book of Esther is God itself. And it's true, his name never appears. But the why of that interests me more. God put enmity between the seed of the woman and the seed of the snake that day back in the garden. But, here, in this story, I believe it crosses again, in the relationship of Ahasuerus and Esther, who he takes to his bed. Who becomes his Queen. Which would explain the absence of

---

[19] It appears that Esther is descended from Saul/Lucifer's brother. How interesting. Think about that. That's not an innocuous bit of lineage, not to this mystery writer. It's a clue. That which came from Lucifer's brother. Who is Lucifer's brother? Adam! As Eve was descended from him. Came from him. Literally. Esther, who is without mother or father, we are told, is Eve.

God. But, make no mistake, God's presence is there. And works magic in this teaching.

As a child in the synagogue, we were told this story every year at Purim. A wonderful holiday, and a most beloved tale of a grand king who's looking for a wife and holds a beauty contest. And guess who wins? The beautiful Jewish girl, Esther. Of all the girls in the kingdom, she's picked. For the rich, goisha' king. Like outta' some Streisand movie. Only here's the catch -- he doesn't know she's Jewish. And she keeps it on the DL, until his nasty Prime Minister, the wicked Haman, appears on the scene, and tricks the King into signing an order to eliminate her people. Esther is then forced to reveal her Jewish identity to her husband to save her people. Lucky for her, the king loves her, and the people are spared. The right girl, at the right place, at the right time. Happy ending. Love conquers all.

Not quite. Here's the real deal. The story begins with a scene of debauchery. The King is throwing a party for all the princes and kings he's conquered. In fact, for everyone in the kingdom. To carouse with him, indefinitely. Celebrate his victories and his ever- expanding empire...His power. He instructs his people to give his guests ANYTHING THEY DESIRE. Anything. Wanna' take a guess who this king is? You only got three choices. Not yet? Here's more.

Six months in, that's right six months in, 'merry in wine', he remembers he's got a wife, the evil Vashti, and suddenly longs for her. He orders that she appear before him and this drunken horde of men, wearing her crown. The fact the crown is singled out, the inference is likely, only her crown. So, they all could admire her beauty, see what a lucky dog he is.

But Vashti refuses to come, probably pissed that she hasn't heard from the cad for six months, or perhaps she objected to the tawdry request. Or, as legend has it, she was leprous, symbolically, the disease of the unclean, and wishes no one to see her marred nakedness. Or possibly, it's her way of twisting him, getting one up on him, controlling him. Kind of like a biblical screw you. That one gets my vote. Based on what we do know of her and her lineage, I believe she symbolizes the fourth character in this drama, Lucifer's other love in this myth, perhaps his great love, the dark feminine, his counterpart, his companion. That's got him coming and going.

We don't know a whole lot about Vashti, unless we turn to the ancient Rabbinical commentary known as the Midrash, and none of it's good.[20] But limiting our study to what we do know biblically, I learn that once again, these stories are connected, and that she is the granddaughter of King Nebuchadnezzar, the King of Babylon discussed above, who brutally conquered the people of Israel, took them into exile, including Daniel, obliterated the Temple built by Solomon along the way, and came up with his own death by fiery furnace. I also learn that her father was his grandson of Nebuchadnezzar, the dissolute Belshazzar, famous for a party he threw where he commanded the drunken revelers to "drink from the holy vessels of the Hebrew Temple" that his grandfather had stolen, "while praising the gods of gold and silver, bronze and iron." Belshazzar dies that night, loses his kingdom to the

---

[20] There she's described as nothing short of cruel, particularly to the Jewish women who attend to her, by her order, not only on the Sabbath, but naked to boot. To complete their humiliation.

conquering Medes, but not before a mysterious message appeared on a wall. He watched helpless, terrified, as a disembodied hand— a kind of *paranormal biblicus* -- scribbled the notorious message:

"mene mene telel upharsin."[21]
Translation: "Your days are numbered. Thou art weighed in the balance and found wanting."[22]

Literally the writing on the wall, the genesis of that expression. A judgment from the great beyond. And, his daughter, Vashti, was taken prisoner that night, as bounty, booty, for the conquering heroes' son, Ahasuerus, the drunken king from our story, to be his wife, in an attempt to unite the vanquished with the victors, under a new king. So, given all that, she might hold a thing or two against him.

Or, maybe, that's the just the way she rolls.

But Vashti's plan – her refusal to appear -- backfires. The King is livid and the men in the kingdom persuade him to give her the boot. After all, what will become of their little fiefdoms of domestic bliss if such "rebellion" is allowed to ensue, and her refusal goes unpunished? Ahasuerus in his fury either executes or banishes his wife – likely the former – only to fall into a deep depression once the liquor wears off, and he realizes his beloved Vashti is gone. So, the men who compose the inner circle cheer him up with an idea of a contest to pick the next queen. They'll round up every virgin

---

[21] Daniel 5:25
[22] Daniel 5:26-27

in the territory, every single one of 'em, bring them en masse to the palace, prepare them for a year with sweet-smelling concoctions, all for a night with the King. He'll bed each one of them and make his decision. And one lucky girl will get to be his queen. Right out of *The Bachelor* fantasy suite playbook. Only in this scenario, the ones "sent home", never get to go home. They remain as his concubines, summoned again in their lifetime should they delight him. Simply stated, every virgin in the kingdom reduced to whores. All for him. Is there any doubt who we're talking about?

Enter, Esther. Of royal descent, I discover, related to Saul through his father. Four years in, and God knows how many virgins later, Ahasuerus takes one look at her, and announces he's found his Queen.

Only then do we find out what's really 'hidden' when out of nowhere, Haman, his prime minister, suddenly appears. Haman, the darkest part of the King, his shadow. The Amalekite. From the line of Agag, the king who Esther's ancestor Saul/Lucifer refused to kill. An evil he refused to eliminate, who lives to destroy Israel from the Red Sea on, now appears in the person of the king's prime minister in this story, who -surprise, surprise -- orders the annihilation of the Jews -- Esther's people – for their refusal to bow to him. The seed of the woman versus the seed of the snake. Her line versus his. Again!

How Esther feels so like Eve to me in her love of Ahasuerus, the guy who looks so good at first blush, handsome and powerful, until his shadow, Haman, appears. A shadow who wants nothing but to annihilate her, and her people. Are you seeing the symbolism? All of it right back to the Garden. The affair, the enmity God set between them, the line of the woman and the line of the snake. And Ahasuerus, wrapped in his own narcissism, his endless desires, his own will.

There's a wonderful Eve/Lucifer moment when Esther's uncle Mordechai, her protector, comes to her and tells her she must act on behalf of her people. She must appeal to the king to save them. She explains she hasn't seen her husband, the king, in thirty days. Thirty days???? They just got married! Some honeymoon. Reduced to little more than a concubine with a crown. And in that passage, we also learn she's not allowed to just appear before him. That if she goes un-summoned, and it displeases him, she's toast. That he holds the power of death over her, literally. Once again, the personification of death. Her uncle, Mordechai sets her straight, real fast. Don't think he'll spare you, sweetheart, this king of yours, this love of your life, if Haman gets his way, the darkest part of him.[23] How Mordechai could so easily be Adam, setting his wife straight as to the true nature of this lover of hers.

I think that, in her heart, Esther/Eve believed that Ahasuerus'/Lucifer's love for her would spare her. That he could never kill her. That he does truly love her. But what would her life be worth, if she were spared? What loathsome value would it have? If everyone, all her people, were dying around her? Could she possibly continue to love him?

And in fact, Ahasuerus does love Esther, and once the plot is exposed, brought to light, Haman is the one who dies. And Esther...the woman... and her people are spared, but in a most peculiar way. The king refuses to reverse the edict he

---

[23] Esther 4:13

signed ordering the death of all the Jews, citing some arcane Persian law that would prohibit such a reversal. Instead, he allows them to defend themselves against the oncoming slaughter. A slaughter, by the way, of his own making.

"That's the last time he'll allow that."

Those words come out of nowhere in meditation, after reading the final passages of this story, just when I'm thinking how he rose up against Haman, that darkest part. Daring to hope. To dream of a happy ending to my own love story. I burst into tears, as once again the Holocaust comes to mind, and the complete and utter helplessness of my people against him. Leaving no doubt that this is indeed a continuing story, in the Bible, in the enmity established in the garden, and in our lives, throughout history.

And something about my relationship with Jack is bringing all of this— all of these characters and stories -- to life. As if these characters are real. In us. It's our story. Not that we're literally these characters. But I cannot deny how much it feels like we are. It's like these characters - these archetypes -- have come alive in us. As energy. Esther to his Ahasuerus. Jonathan to his Saul. Eve to his Lucifer. I'm no longer reading the Bible. I'm living it.

You can go through the Bible using this prism - these three characters -- and it fits. Only then does it cease being disparate morality tales and begin to make sense as a continuous story. Only then does it truly come alive. Hold meaning. Reveal itself. As a love story.

Of God's love for Eve. Wanting her to want him, to choose him. And her love of Lucifer. His pulling her into darkness, into bondage, wanting her to be with him, loving her, having her, but in the process always reducing her to a whore in Jericho, or a slave in Egypt, or a captive in Babylon, or annihilating her completely.

And her husband's redemption of her. Boaz. Moses. Joshua. Judah. Redeeming her. Rescuing her. And ultimately Jesus, teaching her how to break free. Of him. Of death. Of bondage. They're all Adam! He's come for her! That's what this book is about! Not some tribes. And wars. And kings. And idols. And morality tales. No! It's all one piece. One great epic love story! Cover to cover! Her journey into her lover's world, darkness itself. And ultimately her struggle to break free. That's what this book is. Her journey back to Eden. Back to God. It's a story of transformation. Theirs. And a How-to on ours.

Read this way the Bible ceases to be disparate stories, ancestral history, or moral lessons, often misconstrued, but rather a rich, passionate love story. Somewhere along the way, it became a mere tool of obedience rather than a word and story alive with mystery. An epic tale of a love lost, and found. That very well might shape our time here on planet earth, our experiences, our lives. These stories, our stories. Just like the Bible, each one of us, one of these three.

For example, Rahab, in the book of Joshua, the whore, who interestingly lives in the wall of the city, just across from the King. A location of honor, I discover. Primo real estate. The whore next door. In fact, I've come to believe that whenever we see the word "whore" in the Bible, it's a dead giveaway who we're talking about, and what we're talking about -- the woman, Eve. What he's made her. What she becomes in his world. Then, and now. More and more.

I think I got a good friend of mine angry the other day, when he bemoaned his happy arrangement of multiple women he was seeing and sleeping with, suddenly erupting. After all, he'd been completely honest with all of them, and he had. He'd never promised anything -- no exclusivity, totally out front. And he adored them all. How many of us have accepted this kind of arrangement? So like the Samarian woman at the well, drifting from man to man. Bed to bed. All in the name of finding the one. All on the up and up. When did this kind of honesty replace love? What's happened to love?

"You've made them all whores," was all I said.

> "She said, Ye can we get married at the mall?
> I said look you need to crawl 'fore you ball
> Come and meet me in the bathroom stall
> And show me why you deserve to have it all."
> K. West "In Paris"

Hey, I'm no prude, and a fan of the best of Kanye West, moments of true genius. And despite ninety plus percent of the lyrics, a rap fan. But really? Have you listened to what you all say and feel about women? Bitches and ho's is just the beginning, as you crudely announce on top 40 radio what you want to do to them. What they are to you. And it was, after all, my fantasy to make love in a bathroom in France. But it was all about love and passion. Unleashed. Unbridled. It was never about proving my worth. And it ain't no stall.

But it is with him – this energy. It's what turns him on. Not the quality of the woman, but the quality of the body and the booty and the implants. He's made us all whores. Freebies to boot. Props in his own erotic film. And what a film, given the accessibility of porn, and the elevation of the stripper to the desired prototype. It's completely changed the game.

"There's no way that you, young Jewish man from Chappaqua, taught this to yourself,"[24] writer Lena Dunham, creator of the hit HBO series *Girls* cleverly observes. "The first time you see Lena Dunham's character having sex… her back is to her boyfriend, who seems to regard her as an inconveniently loquacious halfway point between partner and prop."[25]

"Do you need me to move more?" she asks…

"Let's play the quiet game," he answers.[26]

Or, the middle-aged, well healed Ira, who hands his cell to his prosecutor brother, Chuck, for a peek on *Billions*:

"God bless these 23-year-olds.
They grew up with porn."[27]

---

[24] Frank Bruni, The Bleaker Sex, Op-Ed, The New York Times, March 31, 2012
[25] Ibid
[26] Ibid.
[27] Billions, Episode 11: "Magical Thinking"

This is his world, more and more. Make no mistake about it. "The Devil is alive, I feel him breathing."[28] Kanye again.

Rahab, for one, is done with it -- his world. She's had it with life under the Luce plan and wants what God is offering. And she fears God. She knows his power. She's heard the story of the Exodus, the parting of the Sea, the fate of the Egyptians. She wants back on the team. She wants to be saved. So, she hides the spies -- these men of Joshua, gives them refuge, safety, protection, on her roof. The roof, once again, the symbol of higher consciousness, the upper room. The highest in her and each of us. Remember Mary, and the angel who told her to get on the roof? This is where Rahab hides these men of God, the advance team who prepare for the invasion. In her consciousness. And covers them in flax. Flax ready to be spun into linen. The garment of the Saints. The requisite garment of a wedding to come. [29]

And in the process of being saved, she sacrifices this king, her king. But then again, what's he offering for her loyalty? A life on her back? He just assumes he's got her under his control, whether by seductive effect, or favors, or fear. But she lies to him, when his men ask about the spies. Plays his game without another thought. Maybe if he'd come to her himself, gotten her back in his power, once again, maybe she wouldn't have lied, couldn't have sacrificed him. Maybe she would have saved him, or tried to. But he doesn't even come to see her anymore. Given the proximity of their living quarters, you get a sense he once did. His consort.

---

[28] "Heard 'Em Say", K.West
[29] Revelation 19:8

Maybe even his queen, some postulate. Now, without him, just a whore.

So, it's far less shocking to find the woman in this story, this whore, in the lineage of Jesus, when you realize that like all the other women in that line, Rahab is Eve, transforming. Breaking free from the king of this world. Lucifer. The pimp. Who must be sacrificed on the way to the Promised Land? Who must die? And how interesting that it is Joshua, Hebrew for Jesus, who saves the woman in this particular story.

She is Daniel to his Nebuchadnezzar. The latter's maniacal desire to be worshiped. To trump God. And Daniel's tender concern for the king that holds him captive, as he tries to warn him, bring him back to God, save him. It's Eve. Again. And Lucifer. Again. No wonder Isaiah's description of Lucifer:

How art thou fallen from heaven, O Lucifer, son of the morning, bright morning star,
Whose desire was to set his throne above the stars of God.

Isaiah 14.

is addressed to this King. Because they are! One and the same! This time as Nebuchadnezzar, who brings Daniel/Eve into his kingdom... into captivity... into bondage. The understanding of who these characters really are, not only gives meaning to their tender relationship, but logic.

She's Jacob to his Esau. Jacob, who dwelt in his mother tents[30], meaning the divine feminine. Who comes out of Rebekkah's womb almost hairless, in contrast to his twin, the hairy wonder Esau, whose heel he holds. Not to get ahead of his brother, as universally preached, forever branded the usurper, the deceiver. No! Not to steal the birthright of the firstborn. He grabs onto Esau's heel as a clue, as to who Esau is!

"He will harm your heel..." [31]

God warns the woman in Genesis, of the snake. Esau is Lucifer! Who threatens and pursues Jacob to kill him. Esau, who cares nothing for the blessings of God! Who sells them for a bowl of lentils – the mourner's stew, symbolically, the food of the dead. Are you getting this? Eat of this fruit and you shall surely die, God warned Adam and Eve. Lucifer is death. Esau dines on the food of death.

Esau who loved this world, the thrill of the hunt. Who married the daughters of the enemies of Israel. Esau, whose line gives birth to Amalek, the great evil that seeks to annihilate at the Red Sea, in Saul, and again in Esther. A line that exists purely to destroy her -- the line of the woman. This is what comes from Esau.

Jacob I loved. But Esau I hated.
Malachai 1:3

---

[30] Genesis 25:27
[31] Genesis 3:15

It all begins to make sense. Jacob. Who ran from Esau, for his life. Who wrestled with the angel in the dark and refused to let go, until he received the blessing. And only then became Israel.

> *He took his brother by the heel in the womb,*
> *and by his strength he had power with God:*
> *Yea, he had power over the angel, and prevailed.*
>
> *Hosea 12:3-4*

> *For the Lord hath redeemed Jacob,*
> *and ransomed him from the hand that was stronger*
> *than he.*
>
> *Jeremiah 31:11*

Jacob is Eve. This is her lesson. Her journey. To struggle against the angel in the dark who she loves, but who hurts and deceives her, and by her determination, her refusal to let go until she receives the blessing of God, only then, and only with the power of God in her, and in her life, does she, can she, prevail against the dark angel. And only then, in this struggle and her willingness, and her determination, is she elevated to Israel, the beloved of God.

Now here's the kicker: The same is true for you. And me. This is our struggle. Our journey.

So, when God speaks of his love for Israel, and her unfaithfulness, it's not that he lost a nation to some idol, some little voodoo doll. No! It's the woman herself that he loved and lost. And her people. To him. The Dark Angel. Her friend.

"Go yet, love a woman beloved of her friend,"[32] God tells the Prophet Hosea in the book of that same name. He buys her for the price of a slave. For she is enslaved. To him. A common whore. Beloved of *her* friend.[33] When I read those words because of my own love affair, I knew immediately what they meant. Who they're referring to. And what she becomes in his world. A slave. A whore. Beloved, or otherwise. The woman, who he likens to Israel there, the adulteress, I believe is Eve. And the Prophet who is told to love her again, is Adam.

Israel. ישראל.The word itself, I learn, encapsulates this story, the verb שרה (sara) meaning to struggle, persevere, persist, certainly recalling Jacob's persistence in his wrestling the angel in the night until he received the blessing, combined with the noun El, an abbreviation for Elohim, a beloved term for God. As in this story, only with the power of God did Jacob prevail. And also, interestingly, closely resembles the union of two nouns – Sarah (once again, the woman) and God[34], adding additional fuel to this passionate fire.

---

[32] Hosea 3:1
[33] "The Hebrew words רע אהבת mean one who loves evil or a friend: because רע signifies a friend, or evil."   Clarks commentary, http://clarke.biblecommenter.com/hosea/3.htm.   While Clark concludes the former makes more sense here, i.e. lover of a friend, I would take exception and say both do, at the same time. For she is the beloved of evil, who happens to be her friend. How interesting that this word translates equally to both.
[34] http://www.abarim-publications.com/Meaning/Israel.html#.UcToSZwaPIU

So, it's no surprise that Jacob/Eve fell in love with the beautiful Rachel, so pleasing to his eyes, just as the fruit was in the Garden. Rachel who refuses to give up the idols of her father, steals them, and lies about it. Beautiful, a liar and a thief. Once more, guess who?

Rachel, who is buried on the way to Ephrath.

So Rachel died and was buried on the way to Ephrath, which is Bethlehem.

Genesis 35:19

Catch that. Rachel is buried on the way to Ephrath, which is Bethlehem. Bethlehem, where the consciousness of the Christ is born. It's not just coincidence that she died there. It's a teaching. This energy that is so pleasing to the eyes, but a liar and a thief, must die and be buried on the way to Bethlehem, where a new consciousness is born. The Christ. In you. You can't take it with you – this dark angel. You can't have both. In my own life, it was Jack or Rio's healing. I couldn't birth this higher consciousness without letting go.

And how telling it is that Jacob's other wife, Rachel's sister, Leah, the "tender eyed", shunned by Jacob in life, in favor of her more beautiful sibling, is ultimately the wife he buries in the place of honor, beside him in the tomb of the Patriarchs, along with Abraham and Sarah, Isaac and Rebekkah. For I believe Leah is Adam, to Jacob's Eve. And Rachel's Lucifer.

Read with these characters in mind, only then can you hear the delicious annoyance in Aaron and Miriam voices in Exodus, as they challenge Moses' marriage to Zipporah, the Ethiopian. Why does he get to marry who he wants? Have whoever he wants? And we get nailed![35]

And Miriam and Aaron spake against Moses because of the Ethiopian woman whom he had married: for he had married an Ethiopian woman.

Numbers 12:1

And how God responds:

"Come out you three," he orders
Numbers 12:4

I would contend, the famous three. And a cloud moves over them, and departs, leaving Miriam leprous. And the passage talks of a father spitting in a daughter's face, a sign of complete contempt, and the shame of a daughter. [36] All for questioning Moses choice of a wife? I don't think so. I think the leprosy is symbolic. The disease of the unclean. The defiled. And the shameful act goes all the way back to the Garden and the shame of a daughter, namely Eve.

Then Aaron said to Moses, not to God, but to Moses:

---

[35] It is, after all, under Aaron's brief authority, and his design, that the infamous golden calf is constructed and worshipped, Exodus 32:1-4, and mass death ensues, Exodus 32:28. And then he lies about his role in creating it. Exodus 32:22-24. Should there be any doubt who he is?
[36] Numbers 12:14

> *O my lord, do not hold against us the sin we have so foolishly committed.*
>
> *Numbers 12:11*

With this new understanding, can you hear his pain? An admission of guilt for a sin, not of questioning his choice of wives, but of a sin foolishly committed, going all the way back to the garden. Can you hear it? Then, Moses

> **Cried out to Jehovah, O God, I beg you, please heal her.**
> **Numbers 12:13**

You can almost hear his love, wounded perhaps... buried. But there for her.

The two men in her life, pleading for her. Interceding for her.

It's almost like Aaron's Lancelot to Moses' Arthur. "Oh, my Lord, please do not hold against us the sin we so foolishly committed." And Arthur, in Moses' appeal to God. "Save her. I beg you. I still love her."

In fact, I wouldn't doubt that this biblical myth is underlying that much later tale set in the magical idyllic kingdom of Camelot. In fact, as I'm editing this section, I have a dream. *Camelot* had been on TV that night, and I glimpsed moments of it surfing the channels. Later, while asleep, there I am as Guinevere holding out my hand to Lancelot, beckoning him to come upstairs, to the upper room, where I say, "You can turn back and see Eden." The dream confirming the theory of a biblical underpinning to that later story. It's them.

And in so many others. A group that would surely include Austen's Wickham and Willoughby to Darcy and Brandon, in *Pride and Prejudice* and *Sense and Sensibility*, respectively, Tolstoy's *Anna Karenina*, or Somerset Maugham's *Painted Veil*, in addition to his *Letter*.

Even *Casablanca*. I mean talk about Christ figures in Victor Lazlo. And the cad in Bogart. That wonderful scene in the beginning with his mistress, Yvonne, as Bogart cruelly blows her off. This gorgeous girl. Destroying her heart and self-esteem. Cagey little bastard. Stringing her along. Hurting her. "What a fool I was to fall for a man like you," she opines.

Yes, he's been hurt. But he's a big guy. Let's call it like it is. He's a player with a past. A smooth operator with scruples, and a heart... somewhere. That found its way to Ilsa. Came alive with her.

"Did you abscond with church funds? Run off with a Senator's wife? I like to think you killed a man," queries the delightful scoundrel, Captain Reynard, musing about his friend Rick. But look more closely at his chosen words. Who is Rick? The thief. The sexual seducer. The murderer. Guess who?

But for her, he's the perfect lover. The man she'll give up everything for. She can't leave him again. She did it once before, out of obligation., she says. She can't do it again. She doesn't have the strength. She'll sacrifice it all for him. I think of my own words to Jesus in the dream from years before. "I gave up a great love once. I won't do it again."

Running to Jack. Falling into that kiss. And I think of Eve, wondering how she felt when she left Eden, separated from her lover. Forced to leave with Adam. Ordered by God to desire only him.[37]

And in Ilsa, Rick becomes a better man. The man we know he is. Beyond honor among thieves. "You're going with him. He needs you. You don't belong with me," he tells her, pushing her away to where she needs to be. At the same time taking up the mantle in his own life, leaving indulgence and nothingness behind, to join the fight, stepping into his own nobility.

All these stories, I believe, have at their heart one as old as time, as Belle would say. Even Belle, who transforms the Beast back into the Prince. Breaking the evil spell. Through love. It's all them.

So, Eve has wrestled with evil, as Jacob, sacrificed it as Rahab, and stood up to it as Esther, where Lucifer failed that test in the case of Saul, refusing to eliminate it. And Adam's test, I believe, his opportunity, comes in the story of Abraham, and the sacrifice of his son, Isaac. After all, Adam

---

[37] I often wondered what their relationship, this marriage was like. Was there love? And for some reason I looked to the story of Abraham and Sarah for answers, to get a sense of their dynamic. Sarah, after all, being the first female following Eve's brief appearance, to get any real page time. Then life—or was it God -- stepped in, and an old friend came into my thoughts, and through the miracle of Facebook, into my life. We talked over old times, and he told me that he never believed the woman he was passionately in love with throughout college, ever loved him. Oh, she needed him, he opined, to lean on, rather than face it alone. Kept him there to take care of her. But romantic love? Other characters and elements of their story and tragic events that transpired were lifted straight out of Eden. At which point, I asked him his Hebrew name. Abraham, he replied. And hers? Sarah. Adam and Eve after the fall. A glimpse into that relationship.

hardly saw what Eve saw in this cat. No falling in love in the Garden for him. So how does God measure... know... that Adam is willing to sacrifice evil? He orders him to kill his son. A son he loved. Who came late in his life. A gift from God. An answered prayer. A miracle. Now there's a test.

But why on earth would I call Isaac evil? Is he?

There's not much written about Isaac in the Bible, I find. He reopens his father's wells that the Philistines have filled with dirt. Some believe the Philistines represent the material world, while others, sexuality.[38] The wells symbolic of the living water Jesus speaks of, that is within each of us, in the midst of us, waiting to be kicked up, and indeed is kicked up in meditation, that heals, regenerates and purifies every cell. Truly taking away the years the locusts have eaten. A veritable fountain of youth. And the dirt, the dirt. You get the picture. Isaac reopens the wells, removes the dirt, all good so far. Even fights with the Philistines about it, and ultimately, they back off. Abimelech, their King, pays him a visit. Abimelech, who had in the past desired Isaac's wife and had come close to making his whore, now offers Isaac a non-aggression pact. You leave me alone, I leave you alone, knowing that Isaac is blessed, seeing the bounty, not wanting to screw with his God, let alone his wife. Not in a

---

[38] Goliath was a Philistine who David slew with a well-placed stone, effectively opening up the third eye in the giant. The stone a symbol of the Christ. To me, that's the ultimate teaching. That the power of what seeks to destroy you will be destroyed by the opening of the third eye through meditation. Delilah sells Samson out to the same Philistines for cash. Using her sexual power to extract from an all too willing Samson the secret of the source of his power – his hair. His hair symbolic, as a Nazarite, of his connection to God and his Divine Power. Her sensuality and betrayal literally cut him off from that Source, and he was left (spiritually) blind. And btw, the same is true for us.

time of famine. No interest in messing with that. Isaac agrees, laying out a feast to seal the deal. Peace among neighbors? Seems that way. Or deal with the devil?

What I found in the ensuing verses is that Isaac forgets the things of God, in this seemingly good-hearted deal. He loses his sight (eyes to see) and is consumed by the feeding of his appetites. And ultimately, in his blindness, wishes to honor that which feeds those appetites, that which seeks to annihilate Israel/Jacob. For the next verse reveals that it is Esau – as in he will harm your heel – who Isaac wishes to bless.

Now Isaac loved Esau, because he had a taste for game
Genesis 25:28.

Isaac, who favors the things of this world, the appetites of the world. Who makes a deal with sensuality: you don't hurt me, I won't hurt you. Who ends up (spiritually) blind, driven by his own primal urges – his love of Esau's wild game. The slaughter of innocent deer.[39] Who's all too willing

---

[39] The deer, so often a symbol of the Holy Spirit or messenger from God, in its gentleness, its absence of aggression. And as the story goes, Buddha as an enlightened being took the form of a deer and offered his life to a king to take the place of the doe that the king was planning to kill. Giving his life in place of the female deer that a king of this world sought to annihilate. Once again, the pattern appears.

I think about Jack's dream of his walking back down a mountain, around the same road he had just ascended. Losing ground. Past a mass grave of deer, caught unaware. Ruthlessly slaughtered. And a fresh kill visible. Right after he had hurt me so. Shut me down. Something dear to him. This 'gift from God." Spirit Slaughtered.

to bestow the birthright on a son who wants no part of it. In direct contradiction to God's word.[40]

This is who Isaac would anoint to lead the nation. And remember what ultimately comes from Esau – Amalek, who for the fun of it, picked off the weakest as they fled Egypt. An evil that threatened to blind the men in the story of Saul – eyes gouged - if they surrendered, otherwise they faced death. Nice guys. And finally, in the story of Esther, evil as Exterminator - Haman. All from this line of Amalek. The line of Esau. This is what comes from Esau. That is who Isaac would seek to bless.

So, it is Abraham's willingness to sacrifice Isaac that I believe is Adam's moment. When evil comes in the form of his own son, benign as that evil is in Isaac, making it even more of a test. As much as he must have loved him, he is willing to kill him.

But how wonderful and perfect it is that God is the God of Abraham, Isaac and Jacob. That it's all inclusive. That God is the God of all three of them. Nothing is left out. No one is excluded. It's not just three names anymore, recited without another thought, mere lineage. No, it has great meaning. It includes us all. It's all God and the God of all. The Faithful. The Prodigal. The Lost. All there is, is God. There is no snake.

---

[40] Genesis 25:23 While still in the womb, God proclaimed to Rebekkah that the older would serve the younger. Esau was to serve Jacob, not the other way around. Rebekkah was forced to resort to a ruse to get around her husband's insistence to defy the will of God and bestow the blessing on Esau. I mean are we to believe that Rebekkah never shared the word that was given to her by God with her husband? Back then? And if not, why not? Or if she did, why did he act according to his own will? I believe it's because of who Isaac is. And who she is.

And lastly, Joseph, adored by his father, Jacob. Remember, Jacob is Eve, so no surprise when you read on who that favorite is.

No biblical story or character is more universally misunderstood by Jews and Christians alike, I've concluded, than this one. Poor Joseph, they say, the father's favorite, persecuted by his jealous brothers, sold, given up for dead. Just like Jesus. Joseph, who takes the peoples' grain in preparation for the famine, and stores it up for later. Smart guy. So far so good. The model of a great steward. And when the famine hits and the people are hungry and come for the grain, he *sells* it back to them – that's right, sells it back to them.[41] Their own bloody grain! When they have nothing to eat! And when they run out of money to pay for food, he takes their cattle, then their land. [42]And finally, their freedom, as they all become his slaves.[43] Jesus, you say? Are you joking?

Joseph, slave to the chief executioner, Potiphar. Ultimately runs his house and all his affairs. The guy who puts people to death. This is who he works for. Death. Are you picking up the symbolism?

Joseph, who dons the robes of the Pharaoh even before he's asked. Cuts his hair. Puts on the ring. In direct contrast to Daniel/Eve, who refused assimilation, refused the food of his king, to dine at Nebuchadnezzar's table – the eating of food symbolic of taking into consciousness. Joseph, who instructs his brothers to lie to the Pharaoh, rather than to

---

[41] Genesis 41:56
[42] Genesis 47:15-20
[43] Genesis 47:21

reveal themselves as shepherds? For the Egyptians hated Shepherds.[44] Hated Shepherds? As in David? As in Jesus????

Joseph who told tales on his brother.[45] Had his father's ear. Sound familiar? The great snitch. The accuser. Joseph, who dreamed of the stars and the sun and the moon all bowing to him.[46] Think back to the Garden -- there's only one cat who desired that. Joseph, who takes his people – takes her – the line of Jacob, the woman, into Egypt, into bondage, and ultimately brutal slavery.

Joseph, whose death provides the final note to Genesis, as the coffin is lowered on him.[47]

The personification of Death.

Like a great curtain closing.

End Act One.

Read this way, with this understanding, with a knowledge of who these characters really are, the magnificence of this story, and all the others, as one continuous tale of a man and a woman and a destructive love affair, really comes through. The subtext, the nuance, the meaning, the passion. The drama.

As in this story, when Joseph insists, as a condition of the family's survival, that the youngest, Benjamin, be delivered to him. Then, is literally overcome when he sees him, and has to leave the room.[48] Then treats Benjamin like royalty. It's not because they shared the same mother. That

---

[44] Genesis 46:34
[45] Genesis 37:2
[46] Genesis 37:9.
[47] Genesis 50:26
[48] Genesis 43:29-30

explanation only goes so far. It's not like they were great buddies. It's because he's in love.

And Joseph made haste; for his bowels did yearn upon his brother.

Genesis 43:30.

This notion of bowels yearning for another is seen again in the relationship of David and Jonathan that led to endless speculation as to the nature of that relationship, until one views it through an Adam and Eve lens. But even more telling are the lovers in Song of Songs – that tale of romance and passion written by Solomon.

My beloved put in his hand by the hole of the door, and my bowels were moved for him.

Song of Songs 5:4

It even reads hot. So, what do we make of the bowel yearn in Joseph towards Benjamin? Sexual longing? Between brothers? Really?

And brotherhood surely does not explain what comes next, when Joseph plants the vessel of divination[49] in Benjamin's bag, and then apprehends the departing crew, proclaiming that whoever has stolen the cup would be Joseph's slave for life. [50] Are you hearing that? His slave. The

---

[49] A vessel of divination is one that tells the future, a practice specifically forbidden by God of his people. Deuteronomy 18:10 And, the future is in fact foretold, contained in Joseph's threat. For the Hebrews did, indeed, shortly after his death, become slaves for life.

cup naturally is found with this brother who his bowels yearn for. Benjamin is Eve. Joseph is Lucifer.

And Judah is Adam, who begs for the release of his 'brother', for it will kill the father if Joseph takes her, and enslaves her. The "father" that it will kill if he loses her is literally Jacob, Benjamin representing all that's left of his passionate love affair with Rachel, the thief. But, I also believe, the father it will kill if he loses her again, this time in the form of Benjamin, is God.

Benjamin, "The beloved of the LORD" who "dwells in safety...between his shoulders."

Deuteronomy 33:12

Does anyone else find that intensely romantic? To lie between his shoulders. To be loved that way.[51]

"Take me instead"

Judah pleads with Joseph. In place of Benjamin. In place of her.[52]

"Take me instead"

---

[50] Genesis 44:17
[51] Or, in the alternative, the tribe of Benjamin that lies between the Northern Kingdom of Joseph, and the Southern Kingdom of Judah. Once again, Eve, caught between them, husband and lover. The favored southern tribe of God, and the lost, of the North.
[52] Genesis 44:33 "Now therefore, I pray you, let your servant abide instead of the lad a slave to my lord"

And with that, I believe, he sealed his fate. On the cross. He paid the price for her, in full. He gave himself for her, this lion of Judah. Put himself in her place. Tears come again from somewhere deep, as I truly feel he gave his life for me. In a deeply personal way. Not for some amorphous sin that I was born with. But for this love affair. This foolish, painful, passionate love affair.[53] He bought me back from death itself. Paid the ransom. With his life.

> *"I'm sorry, Yahweh"*

My earlier dream comes back to me, and the meaning of my apology, ever more clear.

> *"My God, My God, why have you forsaken me?"*[54]

Jesus cries out from the cross, at or about nine the verse reads, nine being the number of judgment. Was the cross also a judgment, a punishment for the sin committed in the Garden so long ago? In my heart, I believe it was. And with this act, he paid the price for his, Adam's sin, as well as

---

[53] And how interesting that the extra piece of land that Jacob gives to Joseph is the very land Samaria where Jesus travels and meets the woman by the well, who has gone from man to man in marriage -- Abandoned? Discarded? The newest guy not even bothering to marry her. Eve's life in the land of Joseph/Lucifer. Reduced to a whore, and a free one at that. John 4:16-17

[54] In Aramaic, the language of Jesus, what he proclaimed on the cross, "Eli, Eli, lemana shabakthani!" , more accurately translates to 'This is my Destiny!' George Lamsa, *Holy Bible From Ancient Eastern Manuscripts*, Matthew 27:46. What I find most interesting is that both are true.

Eve's. Or was the cross, as above, about his love for her? Giving himself in her place. Paying the ransom. Buying her back from Death. Bringing her back from Death.

Or resurrection? Teaching her how to break free. Of him. The snake. Of pain. Of bondage. And death. Teaching us. To break the cycle that began in the garden. The perfect circle. How the story began, when death entered the story. And how it ends. Overcoming death.

Or, all of the above? That it's all one story. That's got my vote.

He's come back for her, this woman he loves. To show her – to teach her -- the way out of this mess. I want to run into the synagogues and shout, "You stopped reading the story half way through! Don't you want to know how it ends???!"

"Woman," he calls to Mary at the wedding at Cana, where he turned the water into wine. [55] And again from the cross. What an odd way to address your mother, and people have bent over backwards trying to explain it, until you realize that the woman, is the woman, Eve. To his Adam. You can feel this in the ease of their relationship, these partners in crime. And partners in redemption.[56] [57]

---

[55] Symbolic of the living water Jesus speaks of, within each of us, transformed into Spirit when it is kicked up in meditation and prayer, and the Christ is born within us. As he says, we are born first in water, as a babe in the womb, and then again, in Spirit. Twice born. Spiritualized.

[56] And I also feel that Jesus not being the son of Joseph has meaning, symbolically. Jesus is not the son of Joseph, considering who Joseph was symbolically. I don't think it was by accident that Jesus human "father" is called Joseph, any more than I think that it's a coincidence that the women in Jesus' life who he loves, are all called Mary. The mother and the woman he loves, one and the same. Eve.

And Magdalene. As a screenwriter, I could see and hear and feel the love between them, when she saw him at the tomb after he had risen, calling her once again, "Woman". And a finish that still makes me cry:

Woman," he said, "why are you crying? Who is it you are looking for?"

---

[57] I believe the Catholics are right in this regard that it was a co-redemptive act that happened in the birth and death and resurrection of Jesus. In a guided meditation, I saw a little lamb who met me as I embarked onto a mountain, and wondered, what's this little guy doing here? The landscape was all very Golden Book —daisies sprouting, trees, flowers, the lamb scampering at my feet. I went on my guided "journey" and when I was ready to depart, there he was again, at my feet. And I heard:
"Mary had a little lamb
Whose fleece was white as snow
And everywhere that Mary went
The lamb was sure to go."
Then,
"Mary, through her divine union with God
Gave birth to the Christ
And it follows you wherever you go."

Through her Divine union with God. A consciousness was born. The Christ. The Messiah. In Mary. And in each of us. If we choose. Was it a Divine Birth? Was he the son of God? Absolutely. I say this without equivocation, as a result of the words I heard that day -- "through her Divine Union with God", and a riddle I heard one morning on waking, barely conscious. My own Riddle of the Sphinx:

"What happened the only time a woman was born with only a man involved?"

Eve, I thought. She fell.

"What happened the only time a man came into this world with only a woman involved?"

Jesus, I responded. He rose.

I laughed.

> *Thinking he was the gardener, she said,*
> *"Sir, if you have carried him away,*
> *tell me where you have put him,*
> *and I will get him."*
> *Jesus said to her, "Mary."*
> *She turned toward him and cried out, "Rabonni!"* [58]

Now it's her turn to rise, repent, turn away from the world. To redeem herself. It's her challenge this time. Her work. To prepare herself. To transform. To die to herself. He's shown her the way. Now she must choose. Who shall she serve this day?[59] We are at this moment in the story. The Divine Feminine is rising. In the story. In the world. And, in us.

She is Eve, Magdalena, the Samarian woman at the well, Ruth, Esther, Rahab, Sarah, Rebekkah, Daniel, Jonathan, Jacob, the Divine Mother, it doesn't matter. They're all the same. They're all her.

She's choosing him this time. It's what she wants. She's had the other. Like Rahab, she's choosing God, she wants back on the team. Like Jacob she's wrestled against the dark angel overpowering her, proving to God her refusal to give in, to let go, until she receives the blessing. And only with

---

[58] John 20:15-16
[59] Joshua 24:15 "choose you this day whom you will serve; whether the gods which your fathers served that were on the other side of the River, or the gods of the Amorites, in whose land you dwell: but as for me and my house, we will serve the LORD. The Gods on the other side of the River, represent bondage to him. And the Gods of the Amorites, the worship of evil. It's no small choice.

God's help, only with the power of God, does she, can she prevail.

And finally, like Ruth, she comes in from a foreign land seeking redemption.

And he (Boaz, the kinsmen redeemer) said, Blessed be thou of the LORD, my daughter: for thou hast shewed more kindness in the latter end than at the beginning..." Ruth 3:10 (parentheses supplied)

What could Boaz possibly mean in what he says, to this woman he just met? But when you realize who they are, and replace Ruth with the Divine "daughter" Eve, and Boaz with Adam, it becomes clear. Even heartbreaking. She is showing the desire for him at the end of the story that was missing between them in the beginning. He means exactly what he says. She had to fall in love with the other, and experience the pain of that relationship, to know what love is not. And what love is. And to want the love he's offering. This new kind of love.

This book is Eve's journey back to God. And ours. At the end, the final chapter, in the wilderness, rising in consciousness. Fully awakening. Getting ready. For her marriage to him.

Let us rejoice and be glad and give him glory! For the wedding of the Lamb has come, and his bride has made herself ready.

> *Clothed in fine linen, clean and white: the righteousness of the saints.*
>
> *Revelation 19:7, 19:8*

There's gonna be a wedding. The remarriage of Adam and Eve.

That is, the risen Eve. Wisdom. The Bride of God.

And the risen Adam. The lamb of God. Jesus.

> *The Alpha and the Omega, the First and the Last, the Beginning and the End.*
>
> *Revelation 22:13*

The first to be created and the last to arrive. The beginning and the end, literally. Nothing more complicated than that.

She, the sister-bride. From the one father, God. The one he lost, to him.

> *You have stolen my heart, my sister, my bride, you have stolen my heart with one glance of your eyes.*
>
> *Song of Solomon 4:9*

Is there an Eve out there in some cosmic realm, or here, actually getting ready? Or is it each of us? Our souls. Are we the Bride? What Jung would call the Hieros Gamos, the sacred marriage of Soul and Spirit. Is that what this is all about? Are all these characters in us? Coming in from a foreign land, this world of darkness, wrestling against the dark forces that seek to imprison us? Working our way through the journey to a union of our individual soul with Spirit? Is that what we long for? Does this explain the emptiness we feel inside – the hole so many speak about -- that we dull or fill with drugs, alcohol, sex, food, relationships, work, or just plain busyness? Is this biblical story, in toto, our journey? Our soul's journey? Seeking union with God?

And, does it go beyond even that? Does it actually provide the framework for the story that is unfolding in each of our lives here on earth? Are we living her journey? Or Lucifer's? Or Adam's? Is this tale playing out in our individual lives, like, for real? Way beyond any morality tale, are we actually living it right now? Each one of us, one of these three? Does that explain so much depravity? Incest, rape, murder, addiction, betrayal. Abuse. Heartbreak. If you've drifted between bad boys and nice guys -- hurt by one, but inextricably drawn, while rejecting what is good for you -- is it this tale? Or, why a woman caught in an abusive relationship will return time and again, defying all rational thinking, especially her own. Sexual slavery, sexual trafficking. Does this story underlie these heartbreaking events? The annihilation of the woman by the snake? I believe it does.

And could it possibly be playing out in the collective – on a whole other level-- in the world story, as well? Is this mythic story – this cosmic tale – in full play, in this realm? Of good guys and bad guys, heroes and saints, magic and treachery. More and more it's starting to feel that way. As our skies grow darker. We all have this sinking feeling that something is up. Could that something be this? Playing out, here? Right now?

And if it is, where in the story are we?

I dream that a tsunami comes and destroys everything.
But somehow, I survive.
Then, a beast from the sea, a stingray, attacks me from behind.
I feel myself die, disintegrate, but still, I'm all good.
In the dream, as I go to sleep, to the sound of gunfire and a war raging, as the darkness falls,
I remember thinking,
"I need a new pair of jeans and a backpack, cause I'm Linda Hamilton in "The Terminator"
and I gotta' look the part."
Sarah Connor --the woman who gives birth to the child who will save the human race.
The next morning, I awaken to what should have been total devastation.
But instead, the world had been replaced.
The old had given way to something new.
Something beautiful.

Chapter 13

The Flood

I move away from the beach. I have to. It's the only way to get away from him. To break the spell. I can't see him every day and stay away. It's a powerful energy that keeps me there, and a destructive one, that's got a hold of me. But a far more serious one that's calling me. Trying to take me somewhere. Show me something. Teach me something. An energy that continues to lift me, and fill me with joy. That's kept me happy, in spite of it all.

So, when the show ends, rather than hustle up another gig, I begin to draw down my pension from the Writers Guild long before it would otherwise become due, and move away from my beach, "to the other side", as Jack called it that day, years before. Just across from the rocks where I first fell in love. Now the ocean will separate us.

Playa del Rey is a little burb stuck in the 50's. Quiet, out of the way, isolated. You enter it through wetlands, and that day in April when I drove in, the wildflowers were in bloom, a blaze of color. I found a great mid-century apartment with a fireplace and a huge deck, packed up our belongings and moved us into our new digs, along with a roommate, that made it all financially possible.

David.

No one could have been more surprised than me. But before making the move to Playa, we spent a month camped out on the canal. After not really speaking for two years, other than to pass him a check each month, or extra cash, we found ourselves living together in the cottage once again. It was hell. The place was a mess, dirty dishes and newspapers everywhere. I didn't know how, or where, to begin. I slept on the couch, surrounded by boxes, suitcases, crap and my treadmill. With no job, I couldn't afford to keep up two places, so here we were. David was in about the same shape as the place, still not over the separation, but less hostile. And recently, he had received notice from the heir to his landlady, that she and her husband were moving to L.A. and had fallen in love with the rose-covered cottage. David had to get out. So, there we were, with the show over and neither of us having a place, and with the bulk of the money gone, having supported two households over the years, two vagabonds.

After checking out some places on our own, we came up with a plan, to pool our resources and live under one roof, as roommates. Separate rooms, separate lives, but helping each other. Supporting each other. Oh, so modern, but a family. Especially for Rio. I'm not going to tell you it was easy or ideal, but it, and he, gave me a way to live the life that was calling me. And I will always be grateful to him for that. And he went through an incredible transformation of his own during this time. Not that he believes in any of this. But he put his life in order. And he stopped drinking. God had a hand in that -- an illness played a large role. But, he was smart enough to listen and slowly returned to the sweet man everyone knows him to be. And I knew him once to be. And work came for him, as a writer. As well as a true calling. Advocating for other kids like Rio, tirelessly, as he had done for our son.

Most of all, it gave us an opportunity to be kind to one another. Definitely a work in progress, for both of us. He remains my greatest challenge – he can trigger me like no other - thus, in new age parlance, my greatest teacher. And friend. And I began to believe, in some odd way, that at least for this moment, it was exactly where I was meant to be.

So, I left my six-figure lifestyle, held a very tony garage sale, where we sold and gifted china and glassware and artwork collected over the years for nickels and dimes, and made the move to the new place. And after a month at David's living in complete chaos, having my own room, full of sunlight, with sliding doors opening to a balcony hidden by perfumed trees, was all I needed, even if all I had in the way of furniture was a beautiful desk and that mattress on the floor, once again. Life literally stripped down and simplified. And I loved it.

I made some half-hearted attempts to find work before I left. A few resumes, interviews, meetings. But truth be told, at every interview I was prone to talk about all these experiences, to testify to all these Hollywood types, that God really exits. No, kidding, I mean *really* exists! *Hey, I'm you! I wasn't seeking squat!!*

No surprise, no offers.

But I didn't care. It didn't matter. 'Cause it became quickly clear where I wanted to be. Right here, in the wilderness. Hanging out with a great, very cool new friend. God. I never thought I would talk in terms of a friendship with God. But as this story continued to unfold, I began to see God as the great storyteller that he is – I mean, have a look at the story unfolding around us right now. As so many have said of late, "You couldn't make this stuff up." And sunsets became his works of art. And falling asleep on the beach under a blue sky felt like sleeping in his arms.

Still, I miss Jack. He's in my thoughts and in my dreams. With her. Blinded. Calling to me. Separated by a wall. Running to each other. But I don't go back. Much as I long to. Knowing he's there every morning. And another day becomes another month, another year. And a certain sadness accompanies the change of seasons. I blow out the pain and longing, and in its place, on the beach, love rushes in and fills that space. Healing me. Loving me. And without realizing it, in this process, something happens. Something changes, in me. Something dies. And something is born in its place. A more authentic me. Solid. Happier. Playful. Full of joy.

"This is the way you're supposed to feel all the time,"

I remember the voice saying it to me that first day. It was good on its word.

The first person I meet in my new home was the cable guy who came to install our computers. We had waited days for the appointment, and by now all three of us hovered on the verge of a nasty internet withdrawal. But when he showed up, the order was all wrong, and he lacked the necessary equipment. He called the office to reschedule. Bad news. It would be another week. He asked to speak to a higher up and put me on. Rather than get angry, I told them how lovely the repairman was. He was, couldn't have been nicer. And in response, the boss gave us three months free, waived the installation fee, and sent our technician back the very next day. Only then did I learn his name. Nehemiah. I had no idea who the character was, but somehow I knew it was biblical. I laughed.

Nehemiah. Cup-bearer to a king. Likely, the very same king as in the story of Esther, I come to learn. The carousing Ahasuerus. Whose father had freed Nehemiah, and his people from the Babylonians, but now his son held him in his own power. But nonetheless, a king who loved him enough to allow him to return to Jerusalem, his home. A city that lay in ruin. That was vulnerable to attack by the enemy. So, that Nehemiah could lead the rebuilding of its walls.

I knew the meaning immediately. I'd left a king of this world, gone to the wilderness to rebuild the walls of a holy city that lay in ruin, within me. My Jerusalem. My soul.

I never thought of my soul that way. As something that needed rebuilding or protection. I just assumed it was a part of me, hangin' around till I died. I also assumed I had lived a good enough life to escape any truly hellish consequence, not that I gave it any thought. But a living breathing vital organ that required my attention in this life? Never.

Jung talks about the first fifty years of our lives being about the ego and the personality -- making our way in this world, obtaining success on its terms. The last fifty, however, he posits, are for the soul – its journey. I can't attest to his sense of timing, but on my 49th birthday, something called me, wanting to be heard and nourished and fed. And in the wilderness, in meditation, in communing with the God within me, like the Hebrews before me, I received that nourishment, that manna from heaven that fed me, that fed my soul. That Jesus would refer to as the food the world knows not of. And a cleansing, like a shower for my soul, and every other organ I might add. I'd never looked younger. A veritable fountain of youth.

I came to this place...the wilderness...on my own volition. But like Nehemiah, I discussed it with a king that I'd served, in a way. And he let me go. And like my king, Nehemiah's wanted to know when he would return.

And in both cases, the person who had fed the king his Spirit – his connection - the cup-bearer of Spirit—was suddenly gone. And with that, his connection to God.

I dream that I'm at work at David's Bridal.

In truth, I decide to dabble in the wedding business and take a part time gig as a wedding consultant, dressing brides at David's Bridal, helping them prepare for the big day. So, in a funny way, with the new job and the move, I've become David's bride, yet again. And mythically, I'm dressing the Bride, which I come to learn has great significance.

In the dream, Jack comes into the shop with the girl from Cuba, who's small and dark. It appears there's a contest going on. The prize? An actual gown in the store that I affectionately call 'The Bride of the Sun', due to its unique sequined pattern that resembles the rays of the sun. It also appears that I have control of the contest and that Jack wants to be sure the fix is in. That the Bride of the Sun is his. In the dream, I tell my sister that Jack's taking his access through me, and that I want to change the access code, from the number 7 to the number 3.[60]
My sister agrees, and presumably, I make the switch. For when I leave the shop at the end of the day, he's waiting there
for me, alone this time, with a gun. Leveled right at me.
I tell him he can't do it.
That he can't kill me. Because he loves me.
I don't know if he fired in the dream. But I do know, I didn't die.

I hit the computer as soon as I'm awake and Google: "Man attempts murder & Bride of the Sun," and I'm immediately led to the Bible. The last book. The final book. The big wrap up. Revelation. A book I had never laid eyes on. Chapter 12, to be exact. The prelude, I come to conclude.

---

[60] Seven representing completion. It is done! And 3, a holy number representing God, as in the triune nature.

And there appeared a great wonder in heaven,
a woman clothed with the sun.

Revelation 12:1

Just like in my dream -- the gown with the pattern of the sun. The woman, the bride, clothed in the sun.

At that very moment, Rio was hooking up with a band. They were arguing over the name. They wanted to call it 'Sons of Rio'. He wanted 'Suns of Rio'. They won. But the message was clear. The two were meant to be interchangeable, symbolically.

So, there appeared a woman clothed in the sun/Son, as in, Divine Son. Wrapped in the consciousness of the Christ.

Then being with child, she cried out in labor
and in pain to give birth.

Revelation 12:2

It's so clearly Eve, yet again, right out of Genesis. And God's admonition that she would suffer in childbirth.[61] Only now, she is this woman clothed in the Son.

And there appeared another wonder in heaven and
behold a great red dragon.

Revelation 12:3

---

[61] Genesis 3:16

And the dragon stood before the woman to devour her child as soon as it was born.

Revelation 1:4

Eve again. Genesis again. And the enmity God set between them, *between your seed and the seed of the woman.*"[62] And Herod comes to mind, the king of Judah, installed by Rome, who I discover, at the birth of Jesus, left nothing to chance as he ordered the slaughter of the innocents – "devouring" all Jewish boys in Bethlehem and the environs, under the age of two. Just to be certain that this new born King, this King of the Jews,[63] this threat to his worldly power, be eliminated. Three guesses who Herod is?

And she brought forth a man child, who was to rule all nations with a rod of iron: and her child was caught up unto God, and to his throne.

Revelation 12:5

Mary this time. The Divine Mother and the Original Mother, seamlessly moving between one and the other, interchangeable. No surprise there, when we realize they're one and the same. And Jesus. And an overwhelming sadness comes over me at the thought of his death.

And, in my own life, of giving Rio to God to heal. And how Jack's presence appeared to devour that.

---

[62] Genesis 3:16
[63] Matthew 2:16

And the woman fled into the wilderness, where she hath a place prepared of God

Revelation 12:6

Just like I had. To the beach. To the beautiful place that God had prepared for me. To a life that was simpler and quiet, but enchanted. Where the best things in life truly became free. That's calling all of us. Each, to our own wilderness.

And there was war in heaven, and the great dragon was cast out,
that old serpent, called the Devil, and Satan, which deceiveth the whole world

Revelation 12:9

Wow. So, the dragon and the serpent are one and the same.[64] The Serpent, The Devil, The Dragon. Satan. It's all him. And there's a war in heaven. And he's cast out.

neither was their place found any more in heaven.

Revelation 12:8

---

[64] Only later do I discover that Greek for the word dragon, (the language of the New Testament from which this was translated), *drakon*, also means serpent. Carl G. Jung, *Man and his Symbols*, (Doubleday, 1964) p.74

And when the dragon saw that he was cast unto the earth,
He persecuted the woman which brought forth the man child.

Revelation 12:13

Loses his place in heaven, his connection. Tossed out. And goes after the woman. When I first read these passages, I could almost hear his plea, "Eve, help me. God's cut me off." But, actually, it says persecuted. He certainly tormented me and tried his unconscious level best to hurt me, if not annihilate my Spirit, but I never doubted for a moment that he didn't love me. And I think of my own surprising words to him, long ago, "You've lost your connection to God." And this latest dream of cutting off his connection – changing the access code -- his access to God --- that he was taking through me. And his resulting attempt in the dream to kill me.

And to the woman was given two wings of a great eagle,
that she might fly into the wilderness
where she is nourished and protected from the presence of the serpent.

Revelation 12:14

And she goes to the wilderness away from him, where she is nourished and protected. Given the wings of an eagle. I'm suddenly reminded of the vision I'd had in meditation years before, when at my lowest, at the point of the betrayal, I was asked to visualize my relationship with God. And I saw myself with the wings of a great bird, hanging suspended, cross-like in front of the sun. The woman clothed in the sun.

And when he could no longer reach her, he

spewed water out of his mouth like a flood after the woman,
that she might be carried away.
Revelation 12:15

He releases a flood. To kill her. So much for my theories of love. But why is this important? This dream? This war in heaven? An archaic, mythic tale of a dragon and a woman and a flood? This bit of "nonsense"? Written by so many you say, at various times? And in the case of this book, Revelations, oft described by even the most enlightened as something bordering on hallucination, if not downright psychosis? Why does it matter? What relevance could it possibly have? To us?

Because that morning, the morning after the dream in which Jack came for the Bride of the Son, lost his access to God, and tried to kill me, while I sipped my coffee and read this very passage, Katrina made landfall.

And the earth helped the woman, opened its mouth and swallowed up the flood.

Revelation 12:16

And the Gulf became a living hell
.

Chapter 14

And the Dragon Went to War

Revelation. The final battle. The final chapter. Are we in it? Is it possible??? Was Katrina the beginning?

So, many have had this thought over time – great minds. I know that. But, the timing of the dream and Katrina is unsettling. Could this truly be happening now, in our lives? In this world? Like I said, we all have a sickening feeling that something's up. That somethin' ain't right. That something's changed. But is it this story? Of beasts and dragons and a woman and a child. Of natural disasters? And a war, whose genesis dates all the way back to the beginning? Was Katrina the first volley? Could it be?

"Woe to the inhabitants of the earth, for the Devil has come down unto you."

Revelation 12:12

Was Katrina that moment? Are we living this myth, right now? Is our story – our lives -- nothing more than their story? Our journey, their journey? Has this always been true? Have we always been living this tale? Of these three? Individually and collectively? And just don't know it?

Surely the battle we call WWII had at its heart this biblical story, in all its hideousness and fury and hatred, and the enmity placed between them back in the garden. The annihilation of the line of Jacob – the line of the woman, Eve. The mandated yellow Star of David. The killing of David over and over. The murderous rage of Saul, the Serpent, for him. David. Adam.

Less obvious, and more surprising, is the growing body of evidence that Columbus may have been a secret Jew, fleeing a place where being Jewish meant torture and death at the hands of the Catholic Inquisitor,[65] the date of his sailing put off for a day in observance of Tisha B'Av, one of the saddest holidays in the faith, commemorating the destruction of the Holy Temples of Jerusalem, first by the Babylonians, the second by the Romans. Placing the actual date of departure on the final day for Jews to flee or face a

---

[65] We were taught that Columbus was from Italy, but he spoke no Italian, rather Castellan Spanish, the Yiddish of the day. Further evidence is the appearance of the Hebrew letters bet-hei on his handwritten correspondence to his son, Diego. Observant Jews have for centuries have added this blessing to their letters, b'ezrat Hashem, meaning "with God's help". "No letters to outsiders bear this mark, and the one letter to Diego in which this was omitted was one meant for King Ferdinand" adding to the speculation of his hidden faith. And finally, the cryptic anagram found on his will -- a triangular signature of dots and letters that resembled inscriptions found on gravestones of Jewish cemeteries in Spain. "He ordered his heirs to use the signature in perpetuity, believed now to be a cryptic substitute for the Kaddish, a prayer recited in the synagogue by mourners after the death of a close relative. Thus, Columbus' subterfuge allowed his sons to say Kaddish for their crypto-Jewish father when he died." All very interesting. Quotes and all material taken from **"Was Columbus secretly a Jew?"** By **Charles Garcia**, Special to CNN, Thu May 24, 2012,
http://www.cnn.com/2012/05/20/opinion/garcia-columbus-jewish

gruesome ethnic cleansing. Coincidence? For certain, a journey financed in large part by Jews, and/or money confiscated from them by Isabel, as they fled, or bribes paid to her in the hope of a respite from the nightmare that suddenly surrounded them. A journey taken in the hope of discovering a new land. A safe haven for his people? Perhaps. Based on the evidence. Surely, a land kissed by God. And, interestingly one that would ultimately be grounded, hundreds of years later, in Freedom of Speech, Assembly, Religion.

So, if indeed Columbus set sail for a better life for his people, better still for all people, his dream was realized, hundreds of years later.[66]

The idea that this biblical myth is fueling the events of our lives and our history, makes the letter from the first President, written to the Jewish Congregation in Newport, Rhode Island in 1790, that much sweeter, and redolent with meaning, when Washington assures American Jews that not only their freedom of religion would be protected, but that their safety, guaranteed.

"May the children of the stock of Abraham, he wrote, "who dwell in this land"...
"shall sit in safety"... and there shall be none to make him afraid."

---

[66] But, none of that excuses his treatment and enslavement of natives. Remember, not everyone in the line of Eve, is Eve.

> *fervent wishes for my felicity. May the Children of the Stock of Abraham, who dwell in this land, continue to merit and enjoy the good will of the other Inhabitants, while every one shall sit in safety under his own vine and figtree, and there shall be none to make him afraid. May the father of all mercies scatter light and not darkness in our paths, and make us all in our several vocations useful here, and in his own due time and way everlastingly happy.*
>
> *G. Washington*

"America has prospered because it provided a place for Israel to be safe."

Not Washington this time, but a thought I hear in meditation, long before any talk of Columbus or Washington's letter had surfaced. In addition to America's unwavering support of the state of Israel, I heard something else in that statement, that day. Something much closer to home. That America has prospered because it provided a place for the seed of the woman, Israel, to be safe. As Washington promised, a "place where none shall make him afraid." No longer did they face the brutal anti-Semitism and Pogroms that had swept through Europe, England, and Russia time and again, throughout the Centuries, each account more horrific than the next. But not again. At least not here. Not on these shores. Subtle anti-Semitism, yes, but nothing compared to the horror the line of the woman had faced and would face yet again in Europe, on a whole new level. No, in this country, that kind of race brutality, to our collective shame, would be reserved largely for Native Americans, and later, African Americans and slavery.

"I saw slavery in the city, among the fashionable and the honorable, having observed it first hand, as the daughter of Southern Royalty. There, everything cruel and revolting is carefully concealed from strangers. I have known the mistress of a family borrow servants to wait on company, because their own slaves had been so cruelly flogged, that they could not walk without limping at every step, and their putrefied flesh emitted such an intolerable smell that they were not fit to be in the presence of company."
The degree of brutality for brutalities sake, is shocking" [67]

Angelina Grimke's groundbreaking treatise, *American Slavery As it is.*

I come across an account of John Wilkes Booth, and for the first time see him described as a Hollywood heartthrob, a ladies' man. Engaged to a socialite, with a whore on the side. Amazing looking and charismatic. A bonafide star. Who knew? No one would dare stop him that night when he entered that theatre. Why would they? He had played that stage so many times. The man with two women and a gun, obsessed with killing the man intent on freeing the slaves from bondage. How interesting. The Old Testament story of Egypt and Moses, all over again. As well, I discover, the New Testament: the day of Lincoln's murder, April 14, thought by many to be the same day another came to free mankind was put to death – the Christ. Coincidence?

Even Thomas Jefferson, *Solomon-like* in both his wisdom as well as his appetites. [68] Widely accepted to have

---

[67] Angelina Grimke, American Slavery As It Is "The Abolitionists", The American Experience, PBS
[68] And what of Solomon, the wise "son/sun(sol) of man"? With his thousand concubines, and hundreds of wives, chief among them and most adored of all, the daughter of the Pharaoh --- the Egyptian-symbolic of slavery and bondage. Solomon, who built his house

bedded the slave Sally Hemings, herself a bequest, or perhaps even a wedding gift from his father in law, who had sired the girl with his own slave, Sally's mother, making Sally half- sister to Jefferson's wife. But that didn't stop him from impregnating her at the age of fourteen, he then a man of forty. Evidence would strongly suggest she bore him six children, all to be freed at the age of 21, by a shrewd agreement Sally allegedly carved out on their behalf, at a moment when she could have fled Jefferson and been free. I find it extraordinary that this man who wrote so eloquently on the subject of unalienable rights, endowed by a Creator—

> "We hold these truths to be self-evident, that all men are created equal.... endowed by their Creator with certain unalienable Rights.... among these...Life, Liberty and the Pursuit of Happiness"[69]

would keep anyone in bondage, let alone a woman he bedded, if not loved, desired, sired children with, all of whom became his slaves. That at no point did he consider – did it enter his mind -- that this Woman, his children by her, or any other of his slaves, who he bought and sold to furnish and pay for his lavish lifestyle, were entitled to the benefit of those lofty words he is remembered for, to those unalienable rights of life, liberty, or the pursuit of their

---

greater, higher, larger than the one he built for God. 1 Kings 7:2; 1Kings 6:2 Guess who? Have a look again at Song of Songs. I don't believe he gets the girl in the end, much as they love one another. The Shepherd does.

[69] The Declaration of Independence, Thomas Jefferson. Drafted between June 11 and June 28, 1776. Formally adopted July 4, 1776.

happiness. And while he freed the brother and two sons of Sally at his death, surely giving weight to claim of paternity, she remained his property to the end, likely for fear of his legacy. Bequeathed to his daughter Martha, this woman appropriately named Sarah, died before she was freed. And in a particularly odious turn, in his will Jefferson also freed two of Sally's nephews, both family men, but failed to do so for their wives and children, who were promptly sold at auction to settle the debts of his estate.[70] This man who rewrote the Bible, eliminating all references to the miracles of Jesus, as well as his deity. Gets you thinking.

I'm introduced to Andersonville, the notorious Confederate Prison, and discover a surprising window into what was to come in Europe 75 years later -- The cattle cars, the depravity, the cruelty. But just a hint. A warm up. A try out. It got much sicker before it landed again in Germany and Poland and swept through Europe. Still, I'm struck how evil shows up in similar ways, again and again.

Even school prayer. However you come down on the issue, I found it fascinating to discover that the woman behind the charge in 1960 to declare Bible reading in the public school unconstitutional, Madelyn Murray O'Hair, was such an odious character. Described, years later by her son on whose behalf the lawsuit was filed, as a woman "motivated by a love of hedonism and a need for dominance:

---

[70] Not completely devoid of heart, Jefferson petitioned the Virginia legislature on their behalf to grant them special permission to remain in the State, close to their families, where they worked in the hope of ultimately purchasing them. Virginia law would have otherwise forced their emigration after one year.
http://en.wikipedia.org/wiki/Madison_Hemings

"When I was a young boy of ten or eleven years old she would come home and brag about spending the day in X-rated movie theaters in downtown Baltimore... My mother's whole life circulated around such things... My mother was an evil person... Not for removing prayer from America's schools... No, she was just evil."[71]

Even if you discount the account of his mother by her now born-again son, there's no denying that she staffed her atheist organization with ex-cons, with a preference for murderers, she herself alleged to have misappropriated millions of donations to her own accounts, ultimately murdered by one such ex-con for that money. How interesting that this is the woman – the face – the force behind the elimination of any kind of religious reading in the public schools. Who knew?

Is it all the same energy? From the same source? Just as in the Bible, are these three characters showing up in our lives, throughout history? Is that what was happening then? Is that what's happening now? The eternal battle of the woman and her line versus the snake and his?

Globally, I look out on our own world and watch as women disappear behind burqas. Are refused education. Prisoners in their own homes. Whose movements are severely restricted, under penalty of death. Abused by husbands in cultures where it is not only commonplace, but accepted.[72] Disfigured by acid. Gang raped. Set ablaze.

---

[71] This quote, and all material on Madelyn O'Hair taken from William j. Murray, "The Madelyn Murray O'Hair Murder", April 5, 2011, www.wjmurray.com

[72] http://foreignpolicy.com/2015/05/01/afghanistan-is-failing-to-

Killed for the sake of honor by the male members of their families. Or sold as sexual slaves. Little more than chattel. Used and discarded. Married off by families while still children to middle-aged men. Mullahs even. Holy Men.

In Africa, parts of the Middle East and Asia, female genitals are mutilated to assure marriage, to tame her, deny her.[73] Young girls in Israel, spit in the face by the Orthodoxy for an ankle showing. Stripped and beaten in Malawi for "ungodly dress". Stoned to death in Mali. Raped in the Congo in numbers that are unfathomable. In South Africa, every 35 seconds. Gang raped and held captive by soldiers in Libya. In Afghanistan. On buses or Holy sites in India. And in Haiti, helpless in makeshift tents. Or in a newly liberated Cairo raped, manhandled, groped, humiliated, debased. And in Yemen, all but gone from view. Women, who only moments before stood side by side their brethren in their fight against brutal dictators.

Or in this country. Raped. Murdered. Abducted. By husbands, boyfriends, fellow classmates, strangers. Women literally disappearing every day.

Is the so-called "war on women" more aptly named than we realize, as programs serving and disproportionately affecting women – single mothers – and the least among us -- the poor, women, children, the elderly, the disabled are put on the chopping block by the GOP in the name of austerity and fiscal discipline, while defending and siphoning more

---

help-abused-women . Around 87 percent of Afghan women are believed to have experienced domestic abuse at least once.
[73] http://www.who.int/reproductivehealth/topics/fgm/prevalence/en/
Even in the United States:
http://www.dailywire.com/news/17233/virginia-imam-says-female-genital-mutilation-joshua-yasmeh

and more money to the top? Then, watch aghast as the same party rallies behind a Presidential candidate who brags about sexual assault in the crudest of terms, and gets elected, facing off against a woman. Whipping his followers into a frenzy with cries to "Lock Her Up." Shouts of "Traitor!" Some calling for her death by hanging, or firing squad. Putin's plot against her; his hatred of her. Comey's public vilification. All, the annihilation of the woman by the snake? This eternal battle? While, women, worldwide, react to this new administration who threatens her choices, her body, her people, leading the opposition, refusing to be silenced. Are these events in our lives right now that seem so catastrophic, all part of this story? Evidence that we're living this myth? Where the villain in the story is a narcissist, a liar, a thief, and a sexual predator....and has a thing for the daughter.... Eve.

From 9/11 to the fall of the markets in '08, as Wall Street gets hit, again and again, are we witnessing the fall of Babylon as foretold in Revelation?[74] Does it make a difference when you know that Babylon was nothing more the worship of money-- where gold was God? Not some archaic civilization long ago that happens to be called out in this last chapter for its brutal treatment of the people of Israel. No, Babylon was beautiful and sophisticated – home to one of the Seven Wonders of the World – a garden, no less, that Nebuchadnezzar built for his wife, who missed her home. (Wow, the symbolism in that.) Its culture was advanced and sexually charged. The pursuit of wealth and beauty. Babylon is us. This world. Are we witnessing its fall? Our fall?

---

[74] Revelation 18

Is the nuclear threat of Iran, with its heated anti-Israeli rhetoric, and a President seemingly hell bent on inflaming it; the brutal attacks in the name of ISIS, and the Western response; the hideous war in Syria -- is all this the road to Armageddon, or the new normal? As cries for freedom that sweep the Middle East are followed by chaos and repression, and the rising threat of terrorism and terror cells around the world, and this same President wonders aloud, if we have nuclear weapons, why can't we use them? As North Korea launches another test. Mikhail Gorbachev warns of a world preparing for war. And the doomsday clock is moved closer to midnight.

Is the lack of job creation, gridlock, corruption, globalization, trade agreements – a combo that has already moved millions towards a desperate, dark, next chapter, in a race to the bottom, and the resultant rising inequality, all part of this battle? Worldwide. Leading, to a new brand of right-wing nationalist populism across the world. Angry. Divisive. Racism, Anti-Semitism, and fear on the rise. Along with chaos. The feeling of a world out of control. And America, a once great power, "deconstructed" by this new leader. And the world watches helpless, as it slips away.

Once again, business as usual? An unfortunate chain of events? Or part of the final battle? This final chapter. Where everything has a rational purpose or explanation. Hellfire and Brimstone are not going to rain down on the earth, and people with strange Biblical names appear. No, it's gonna be a lot more tricky, more clever, less obvious.

Until it's not.

Is the betrayal by our Politicians, the betrayal by our men part of this story? The slaughter of the innocents in Newtown? On college campuses? In High Schools across the U.S.? Military Bases. Movie Theatres. Night Clubs. Do they all relate back to this?

Are these events clues that the grand opus is wrapping up, right now, before our very eyes? That we are indeed in the final chapter? Literally living it?

Where relationships, tragedies, catastrophes and events that seem intent on destroying us, are actually serving a purpose? Conspiring to push us, pull us, get us, where we need to go before the story ends?

Before it's too late?

Chapter 15

The Meaning of Betrayal

Our systems and leaders are failing us. Our businesses have abandoned our workers for cheap labor abroad, sacrificing a country, and their fellow countrymen, neighbors, for their own personal gain. Leaving us on a race to the bottom. Talk of the importance of remaining competitive and eliminating the minimum wage. As the number of Americans living in poverty hits another tragic, record high.

While our financial institutions, the very ones who brought on this mess through fraud and greed, go unpunished. Crippling us. Freezing us out. Helping themselves to our Treasury. The People's money. Dumping their toxic instruments that made them rich, at our door. Heads they win, tails we lose. Gorging at the Federal Reserve, while they foreclose on our homes. And the market rises.

And our politicians are bought. Creating safe havens for their donor's cash, tax cuts, and trade agreements, that not only permit this abandonment and privilege, but promote it, enhance it, enable it. Who are these guys, we ask? What happened to our democracy? Even the illusion of it? More and more, America, once the beacon of hope and opportunity morphing into an oligarchy, a kleptocracy. And now, complete with an autocratic tone, that chills.

And it all happened so quickly. It seems like overnight we lost the dream. One minute the promise for each of us, the opportunity to make yourself, unlimited. Strictly a matter of hard work and intelligence. Now gone. In the downturn, Federal and State budgets for higher education gutted to pay for tax cuts, primarily to the rich. Once a way out, college has become out of reach for too many. Others go into crippling debt they'll never find their way out of, reaching for a ring that was once so attainable. Mobility disappearing. Inequality exploding. So many drowning in debt and a job market that has left recent grads and aging workers unemployed, or underemployed. Professionals, managers, skilled laborers, struggling to regain the financial footing they lost in the recession. Literally "Lost in Long Island". Leaving millions, other than the privileged few, to fend for themselves, to feel abandoned, discarded, forgotten. Betrayed.

A Democratic presidential candidate sets our dreams and hopes on fire, comes into office and makes deals that run directly counter to our interests, let alone the sentiments of the majority who put him there, or even his own message. A failed attempt at bi-partisanship? Compromise? Or this story, as malaise sets in, fueled by the betrayal, and too many sit out the mid-terms, then watch in horror as the battle lines are drawn in the now Republican-controlled House and State Legislatures across the U.S., where an assault on workers' rights, voting rights, and women's rights is waged. While nationally, tough talk on entitlements. Internationally, cries for austerity. And more tax cuts for the rich doled out by corrupt politicians. More trade agreements that promote corporate interests at the cost of the American worker, the later all but abandoned. Left to fend for himself. Ultimately leading to a wave of populism, and the election of billionaire Donald J. Trump, and his toxic brew of savior, hatred, racism, fear, and still more tax cuts for those who need them the least, as millions are denied Health Care. By Christians. Brave new world, indeed.

Betrayal. Before Jack, betrayal for me was the stuff of some good, often very bad drama. And Russian novels. Now it was everywhere. Isn't that the way we feel by all of this? Betrayed?

And beyond the politicians, beyond the bankers, and the greed, over the years how many men have we seen publicly betray the women in their lives? Erin Woods, Sandra Bullock, Jennifer Aniston, Jennifer Garner, Rhianna, Gwen Stefani, Miranda Lambert, Huma Abedin, Maria Schriever, Hillary Clinton. The list goes on and on. Beautiful women. Accomplished women. Rich women. Desirable women. Powerful women. The cream of the crop, some may say. Betrayed and publicly humiliated. Beyond the limelight, I meet women every day who have suffered an eerily similar betrayal by men they thought were the one.

What does it mean? Beyond the obvious lessons. Beyond the psychology. Beyond women who love men who hate women. Beyond stop signs... warning signals... mother issues... father issues... red flags... bad choices... even worst choices... the collapse of society... the collapse of the family... the failure of commitment... misplaced values...

the death of romance... Does it have meaning? A higher meaning? Is it all this story?

Knowing what you now know, and beginning to see things mythically, if not mystically, don't you find it interesting that Tiger Woods -- a Tiger in the woods - the animal symbolic of aggressive sexuality, in the dark, dank, primeval forest - hell, it even reads sexual - betrays a woman, whose name Elin means 'the Light'. I mean, come on, you can't make this stuff up. Woods is the aggressive sexual energy who betrays the woman who is light. He is the energy who makes all women whores. Woods cut quite a wide swath, but numero uno? Rachel. Remember Rachel? The great love of Jacob? The woman so beautiful to the eyes, who enchanted him, stole her father's idols, hid them, and lied about them. This is who he sought after, symbolically. Who he's in union with -- Rachel. The beautiful liar and thief. The dark feminine. Lucifer's consort. His great love.

Or Jesse James. This bad boy marries, then publicly betrays and humiliates Sandra Bullock, America's sweetheart. We wonder if he's lost his mind, as his lover du jour is pictured in front of a coffin with a swastika tattoo. Think about it. Put it thru the mythic prism. A betrayer, a coffin, a swastika = the betrayer, in union with death, the same death that seeks to annihilate Israel -- the woman and her seed--Eve.

But before we condemn these men, these pols, these bankers, these CEO's as the demon seed, are they imbued with a purpose? A high purpose?

The story began with a betrayal. When Lucifer betrayed Eve. This angel who dreamed of being greater than God. To sit above God. There to protect these humans, according to Ezekiel. Not to seduce her. And when God brought the hammer down on his lover, there was no *"Hey, this is strictly my fault. The dame had nothing to do with it. She was toast before I even said hello. Give her a break."*

No, Lucifer stood silently by and watched as God cursed them and tossed them out of paradise. And reduced him to a creature who eats the dust, slithers on the ground.

Was it love? Or something more nefarious? A plan on his part that went amiss? After all, he was in the catbird seat before *they* came along. In a jealous rage, perhaps he plotted their demise --to teach this woman the ways of the world, have her seduce her husband, taste the forbidden fruit, and throw them right out of God's favor. But perhaps what he didn't figure, factor in, was her falling in love with him. And his inability to resist her.

But without it -- this betrayal of Eve, of Adam, of God -- there would be no story. No journey. No falling into form. Evolving into consciousness. Finding their way back. Choosing God. Crucifixion. Resurrection. Overcoming Death. Paying the Price. Showing her the way. None of it.

Every great story needs an inciting incident – something that kicks it off. This Betrayal – his betrayal, was theirs.

Could these men, Presidents, politicians, bankers, cads, players, catastrophic and heartbreaking events, betrayals, be ours? In our story? *Our inciting incident?* All in service to a Divine pattern *in our lives*, collectively and individually? *Taking us where we need to go.* Each of us playing a part. Some get the good guy role. Some, the not so good. Deeply entwined, like a magnificent tapestry. Pushing us, pulling us out of this story of good and evil...back to the Garden. Back to God. Out of duality, to the oneness of God. To wake up to a realization of who and what we truly are. Each one of us. Pure Spirit. Every cell. Every inch of us.

And the true purpose of our being here –This journey. This awakening. This realization. The journey of our soul.

"Love thy neighbor as thyself" he taught, because we are! All one. All aspects of the One. In this together. "All there is, is God. There is no snake," God said to me in the dream. It's all God.

I'm beginning to sense that everything in our lives – from hurricanes to heartache -- is a call from the Higher Self to awaken. To take this journey. Our injuries, our hurts, tragedies, disappointments, illnesses, heartbreak, pain, unemployment, betrayals, all of it – are nothing less than a call from God. *That there is Divinity in our worst nightmare.* Just as God used the enemy of Israel to call her, bring her, back to him, time and again in the Old Testament, the same is true for us. That it's all a call. That we're all the Prodigal. On a Divine Mission. Wasting our inheritance. Dining with Swine. That we're all in this together, finding our way back to God. Everyone playing their role. Even Donald Trump. I never thought I'd say this, but is it possible that Michele Bachman is right, that he was sent by God? To wake us up.

*"You can't always get what you want.
But if you try real hard, you get what you need."*

That Stone's tune blared as Donald Trump celebrated his victory late that night. What an odd choice, I thought.

What could it mean? Surely those words were not for him. Winning for him is everything – he got what he wanted. So, who was the song addressing? America? Maybe he wasn't our choice, he seemed to be saying, but it's what, in his mind, this country needs. To rebuild our infrastructure, to right our trade deals, to rid the world of terrorism, establish the best schools. Make America Great Again. And, only he could do it, he proclaimed.

Or, perhaps, it wasn't "America" the Stones' tune was speaking to that night, but rather, to each of us. It may not be what we want. For the 65,844,95 majority, their answer was loud and clear. But could it be, strange as it sounds, in the highest sense, what we need? *In these times of trouble, could this trouble -- this betrayal of everything we stand for -- be our invitation?* Not to a different political party. Or strategy. Or rally. Or demonstration. Call to Congress. Even riot. But, to nothing less than God?

In his wonderful book "The Christian Archetype", Jungian analyst Edward F. Edinger sets forth Jung's interpretation of the Christian myth as a series of events that chronicle the journey of the Soul -- *The birth of the Higher Self in the individual, and the corresponding death of the ego.* That bears repeating. *The birth of the Higher Self and the corresponding death of the ego, in each of us.* That journey, Jung postulates, the journey of your Soul, is, in fact, an exact mirror image of the life of Jesus.

In the work, Edinger breaks down Jesus' life into twelve stages and writes about each stage as it relates to us, to our lives, to our journey. A little more than half way through is the Arrest -- the Betrayal.

Why betrayal? Why in this cycle of the death of the ego, the 'egoic' lower self, and the birth of the Resurrected Higher Self, is betrayal a necessary part? What is it about betrayal – a stage immediately followed by humiliation? Why? The story of Jesus could easily have been told without a betrayer, let alone one of his own. The Pharisees could have worked with the Romans without Judas' help. It's not like Jesus was in hiding, or incognito. Or ignorant of what was to come. In fact, Jesus ordered it. So why? And why Judas? And does it all somehow relate back to Eden? Do all our betrayers? Are they truly our own personal snake in the grass? Including Trump?

Prior to his betrayal of Jesus, Judas, we learn, was a thief, skimming from the collection box. A thief, and a liar, and ultimately a murderer. Any doubt who we're talking about? What's also revealing, I come to discover, is the event transpiring at the moment Judas decides to kill him -- to give him over to a certain, painful death. He's watching as Mary Magdalena falls at Jesus' feet, and with love covers them in her tears, wiping them with her hair, and finally perfuming them with rare, imported, expensive nard. Judas objects to the use of the nard -- it could have been sold for the poor, he insists. Noble objection, until we learn in the next breath that he was dipping into the collection box. So, was he just pissed at Jesus for cutting into his action? Is that the motivation? But killing Jesus would surely put a crimp on all things financial, so I don't believe the primary motive was greed. No, Judas decides to kill Jesus as he watches Mary submit herself to him, with love and reverence. This is the act that sets the betrayal in motion. Once again, as in Eden, three characters -- a liar, a woman, and the son of God

-- the same three characters. And, as in Eden, a betrayal that leads to death. Only this time the woman is choosing Adam – the risen Adam. And this time, Jesus proclaims, death is not the end:

I lay down my life, that I might take it again
No man taketh it from me, but I lay it down of myself.
I have power to lay it down, and I have power to take it again.

John 10:17-18

This time death is the beginning. The Resurrected life. In Jesus, and once again, Jung postulates, in each of us, in our lives. As we die to ourselves, to the small egoic self, and allow the greater Higher Self – our true nature -- to emerge.[75] The betrayal and the accompanying humiliation serve, according to Edinger, "to facilitate the utter degradation of the ego." [76] I can vouch for that. A process, he puts forth, that "belongs to the *mortificatio* phase".[77] You don't' have to know much Latin to understand: Death of the ego. That "the

---

[75] This by-play between the ego and the higher Self, as to who's running the show, and the ramifications of the ego who refuses to make room, is brilliantly discussed in a work by John A. Sanford, Jungian Analyst and Episcopalian Minister, on King Saul. As we look at a nation hooked on Anti-Depressants and Anti-Anxiety medication, his discourse on egocentricity and its relation to anxiety and depression is a must read. "When the Self tries to break through the egocentric defenses we experience anxiety", he posits. "Depression is the opposite. The Self has moved far away." John A. Sanford, *King Saul, The Tragic Hero*, (Paulist Press, 1985) Appendix A, *Depth Psychology Looks at Saul*, p.129-130.
[76] Edward E. Edinger, *The Christian Edward Archetype*, (Inner City Books, 1987) p.91
[77] Ibid, p.91

ego must be *relativized* to make room for the (greater) Self."[78] Make that crushed. Minimized. Pulverized. But in its place, if you answer the call, something is born. Something glorious. And that, I believe, is its purpose.

I often felt, in the midst of the worst of my own betrayal, that I could almost hear God saying, "Well Eve, how do you like him now?" But it took that betrayal, to really see who he was, face to face. It took something that painful, administered by a man I adored, to finally utter a resounding NO. To finally honor myself. And to allow it to take me where I knew I needed to go all along. As I fled from the pain, the betrayal, from him, to the wilderness, and God, I felt like Jonah who had run from his Divine calling[79] choosing instead to head to Tarsus and Joppa – centers of wealth and beauty – gosh, well that could be any one of us -- only to find himself caught in the belly of a great fish, ultimately to be spit out on the very shores where he was called to go in the first place. In my case, to the wilderness where I was called all along. It all took me there. David, Frank, Autism, and finally, Jack. Especially Jack. Had he been kinder, more loving, would I have gone, answered the call? Without the betrayal? Destiny or no destiny? In the end, it was Rio's regression that finally got me out the door. But it was the pain of this betrayal, and the humiliation that followed, that shook me to my very core, and an awareness

---

[78] Ibid, p.91, parenthetical supplied by author.
[79] Hating the thought of Nineveh being saved. Nineveh, part of Assyria, was a gruesome enemy of Israel, brutal in their treatment. You can't blame Jonah for not wanting to warn them of God's coming wrath, wanting to see them extinguished. Jonah, I believe, an incarnation of Adam, who has no interest in saving Lucifer. If that be his calling, he wants no part of it.

that it could repeat, would repeat, until I answered the call, that kept me away.

The betrayal in your life is attempting to do nothing less. To take you here. To this journey. To this calling on your life.

"It is an act of love to lead a person to his proper destiny."[80]

I read and re-read these words in Edinger, and know in every part of me that this is true. That it is an act of love to lead a person to his destiny. This is what the betrayer does in your life, or is intended to do. Leading you where you truly belong -- to the Highest in you. That the ego be pulverized to make room for nothing less than the Greatest in you. To awaken the God in you. Which may explain why the betrayal, in the case of Jesus, "is accomplished with a kiss and why Christ calls Judas "friend" as he receives the kiss....and reacts angrily when Peter urges him to avoid his fate." [81]

It *is* an act of love to lead a person to this transformation. To this destiny. To a place where miracles happen. Where healings happen, to you and those around you. Where magic happens. A place that is mystical. Enchanted. Full of Beauty. Where Joy is experienced for no reason, apart from circumstance. And love. And a peace and a calm that truly does pass our human rational thought or understanding. Where life becomes sweet. He, or she, is your friend, this betrayer of yours who leads you to all this -- the

---

[80] Edinger, The Christian Archetype, p.83
[81] Ibid. p.83

soul mate you think he is, you know he is, or thought he was. Whether he knows it or not, or acknowledges it in this lifetime, he is your greatest fan. Rooting for you to take this journey. Getting you where you need to go, in all the pain, the despair, the withholding of love. Knowing how important it is. That quite possibly your very salvation depends on it. As well as his.

And, if I'm right, and this love story from the beginning is playing out in our lives, and these characters are alive in us, it makes perfect sense, and only fitting, that you must give him up, this lover of yours, and he must sacrifice you. It was, after all, your affair that started this mess. You're in this together. And you must part.[82] You must give him up, in

---

[82] For Biblically, he is Jephthah, the rejected Son of Israel, who made a vow to God and agreed to sacrifice whatever came first from his house to greet him on his return from battle, if only God would grant him victory over his enemy. He got that victory, but at a cost. For on his return, it was the daughter, his daughter, who he loved more than anything, who emerged to greet him. The daughter that he must now sacrifice – as a virgin no less. Hands Off! The daughter I believe, symbolic of the Divine Daughter that he must sacrifice, is you. And the enemy he seeks to have victory over, that he sacrifices you for, is the enemy within himself. He must give you up. That's the deal he made with God. His journey – if not his redemption, depends on it.

And you are Jacob, who buries the beautiful Rachel – so enchanting to the eyes, but a dark energy, a thief and a liar, on the way to Ephrath which is Bethlehem, where a consciousness – the Christ -- is born, in you.
In other words, you must bury him and he must sacrifice you.

I wondered if I was right about all this, and on a particularly blue day, when I questioned every move I had made on this journey, including the craziness of choosing it in the first place, away from the world, the affluence, the career track, my melancholy ultimately drifted back to Jack, and I said to God, if I only knew that this was hard for him as well, that he felt this loss, I could handle the sacrifice, just knowing that. And I opened the Bible to read the Word I had come to love, to crave, the vibration, the cleansing I got every

whatever way he has you. Whatever way he's got you in his grip.

But unlike the Eve of old who was ordered to leave Eden with Adam, and to "desire only her husband", torn from her lover – only to return to him time and again, or be taken by him, and find herself enslaved...in bondage....a whore...whatever... miserable -- this time it's different. It's a wiser Eve. She's aware of who he is. What he is. What he becomes with her. And what she becomes. Oh, maybe when she first leaves and goes to the wilderness she feels the same, missing him, shedding tears. But something happens there, in that wilderness, that feels, for a moment, like death. Dry, like the sand around her. And she looks back longingly at the life she left behind. Not unlike Lot's wife. Or the Hebrews, longing for their life in Egypt, forgetting the bitterness and pain of bondage, remembering only the sweet.[83] But she dares not go back. In part, because she knows nothing's changed. She knows what awaits her there -- more pain. And she knows the story will keep repeating until she follows the greater message and answers the call. She also fears God – yes, this God she loves -- knowing there are consequences for refusing. Consequences in this lifetime.

Like the woman in the Song of Songs, who has washed her feet (purified the sole/soul), gotten naked (as in Eden), but returns to the street in search of this lover that came

---

time it moved through me, washed over me, to say nothing of the mystery that was unfolding in its content, as its true meaning was becoming clear, and my eyes fell on these words:
"And Jephthah made a vow" Judges 11:3
[83] The true purpose of the reading of the Passover story, every year, to remember the pain. To not look back. To not go back. To not turn back. To leave sin – the leaven – behind. To leave him behind.

a'callin, that she longs for, but now these same streets which once welcomed her, meet her with brutality.[84] And, as much as he longs to hear her voice[85], he tells her to turn away from him, for she has overcome him.[86] Each of them knowing that something greater is at play in her life, and his. So, in the wilderness, she cries it out – this pain, this loss. She blows it out. And in its place, a love moves through her, pours into her. Healing her. Loving her.

For at the end, in that day, your men will have nothing for you, God tells the woman in Hosea -- a book I believe is of paramount importance right now – no corn, no wine, nothing. For I want you in the wilderness where I can speak to your heart and minister to you and heal you. And have you in the Earth. Pretty hot stuff. And give you that corn. That wine. And you will know that all the time it was me, working through them.[87]

And it shall be at that day, says the LORD, you shall call me Ishi, my husband
and shall call me no more Baali, my lord.

Hosea 2:16

This isn't about Israel coming back to God from some voodoo idle worship. No! It's about a great love once lost, now found. It's about you. It's about me. It's more than realizing that you were better off with your original

---

[84] Song of Solomon 5:2-7
[85] Song of Solomon 8:13
[86] Song of Solomon 6:5
[87] Hosea 2:6-15

husband – your betrothed in Eden-- then in the world, hurt and betrayed by these other men,[88] a lesson many of us are learning. No, it's more than that. Something happens in the wilderness to this woman – to me, to you -- as he moves through her and has her in that earth, and ministers to her, and, as he promises in Hosea, heals her.

She falls in love.

These betrayals are your invitation to that love affair. To say no to him. No to his world...this world. And, yes to God. To seek God, face to face. Not to some religion, or moralizing, or Church or Mosque or Synagogue. I mean if you connect with God there, great. Do it. Wherever. Mountain top, ocean, living room, your own back yard, I don't care, wherever. But, do it. God is an experience. God is a love affair. Not a belief system, religion, or opiate for the masses, but a tangible, tactile experience.

But don't take my word for it. In fact, my words don't mean squat if you do nothing. You gotta' take the step. *Discover it* -- within you. *Ignite it*—within you. See for yourself. Experience it for yourself. Start your journey. All that crap that's happening in your life right now—all the disappointment, the heartache, the illness, depression, anxiety, the struggle, is trying to get you here. It's screaming at you to begin. To a way of walking in the world. Full of joy. And life. And peace. And love. So, bless it all. Even the betrayal. It all has a purpose.

---

[88] Which the woman in Hosea cops to. Hosea 2:7. Much like the prodigal son in Luke (a magnificent story that will bring you to tears – by all means read it in Luke 15:11-32) as he comes to his senses, and begins his journey home. His prodigal, to her whore. His Lucifer to her Eve.

Go to your wilderness, wherever that is. And see the Presence of God. Everywhere. Really see it. In the sky, in the waves, in the birds, in the beauty. And feel it. In the ground that's supporting you. The gentle breeze that's caressing you. In the sound of the waves or a gull – it's speaking to you. Cry out the pain. The Anger. Blow it out, literally, and breathe in Love. Let it move through you. Then, breathe out peace. And close your eyes and imagine that peace falling like a wave, washing back over you. Feel it. On your shoulders, on your face. Then do it again. That breath, nothing less than the Holy Spirit itself, will heal you, given the chance.

Read something spiritual that lifts you, and close your eyes again. And in the silence, you will begin to feel a love moving through you, a peace moving through you, a light moving through you. And the more you do it, the brighter the light, the stronger the energy. It may not happen immediately. Stay with it. Start each day this way, before you walk out into the world. And what you will find will be as real as anything or anyone in your life. And then, at some point, more real. And you will walk in joy. And your life will change. It will lighten, sweeten. Enchant. And you will change.

And right now, especially now, it's a journey you're being invited, encouraged, implored to take, as our systems and our leaders fail us. As the skies darken, and our future grows precarious. As our men betray us. It's all for a reason.

We're all in this together. We're all being called.

Seek ye first the kingdom of God, and his righteousness, and all these things shall be added unto you.

Matthew 6:33

That's a truth Jesus articulated. A truth that I believe governs the Universe, whether we know it or not, like it or not, follow it or not. And until we do, until we seek God, we will spin in our self-created circles, the Adam curse – the treadmill of life. And our situations will remain stagnant at best, or increase in gravity, as they continue to "call" us. When Jesus came, he didn't organize the people against their oppressors, much to the chagrin of the Hebrews. They expected a savior, their Messiah, to deliver them from the cruelty of the Roman oppressor. Rather, he articulated spiritual principle. It was as if he was speaking to Eve – as he spoke to them – this line of Eve -- I could almost hear him. "Sweetheart, let me show you how to get out of the mess we've gotten ourselves into." He was showing her the way. Seek the Kingdom. Go higher. It was if he had the key to this mystery. That this story they were living was part of a larger tale. In service to a higher story. A higher journey, of the soul. The journey back to Eden. To the consciousness of Eden. And the one that's captivated us here -- the journey of the personality – the carnival ride we're on, is a ruse. A lie. And, if we don't answer the call, a trap.

I believe we're in this story. And if my dream about Katrina tells me anything, we're in the final chapter. And running out of time. To wake up. So, do it. Begin. Seek it. God itself. First thing. Everyday. Wherever you choose. But make it sacred. Make it special. Set the time off just for that. One on one. Turn away from the world and turn your attention to God. Deliberately. For no reason, other than to experience it. To make the connection. Read. Uplift yourself. Close your eyes. Swim in that vibration -- that Higher Vibration. The Vibration of God. Hang out there. Cry out the pain and breathe in love. And watch as your life changes. And you change. And perhaps, the world.

For I believe, all of this is meant to take you there, including Mr. Heartbreaker, the humiliation, and the pain. An illness. A betrayal. A world in chaos. And those who create it. All of it. Intended to take you on this journey. To your destiny.

"People say everything happens for a reason.
These people are usually women.
And these women are usually sorting through a breakup.
It seems that men can get out of a relationship without even a goodbye.
But apparently, women, have to either get married or learn something."[89]

Hey, Carrie! I've got proof!

I dream I'm on a grassy hillside, at play with a group of -- I want to call them "maidens." All smaller than me,

---

[89] Darren Star, Liz Tuccillo, Candace Bushnell, *Sex in the City*, "The Post-It Always Sticks Twice." And guess what? It was Mary who was lost at the end of your show, and found. And John, who came for Carrie/ Sarah. Even there, these characters seem to making an appearance.

considerably younger and dressed in a simple garb definitely from another time, circa Braveheart.

In the dream, we're playing with a pale yellow beach ball, the color of the sun. The goal is to keep it afloat, and I think to myself how innocent this all seems. I think I like it – being here, playing this game -- but I'm not sure. At which point, I look to my right, and there, across the field, on an adjacent dirt road, is God. And to his left, about five feet away, Jack. Both of them, watching me.

I don't sense a great deal of love between them, more like a working relationship. In the dream, somehow, I know that Jack is there making a delivery and that he's late. Then suddenly, without asking anyone, most of all God – he's such a rascal -- Jack lets loose of the frisbee he's holding in his left hand -- just like the frisbee he threw to the beloved Max, all those years -- and it sails clear across the field, hitting me smack! in the middle of my chest.

Bulls-eye.

"To sin" means nothing more than to miss your mark.

He hit his. Me.

He made his delivery. Late, but he made it.

To this place. This field.

To God.

He wanted me to see him. To know he was there.

Was he staying?

Hard to say.

But one thing was clear, for sure.

All the time he was working for God.

Chapter 16

The Betrayer

"You're in the grip of a malevolent force. Go to the mountain."

Jack hears this in a dream. He's in flight, on a perilous journey, in the grip of a malevolent force that has a hold of him, his every move. This feels so right...this warning. I'd seen the best of him. I knew that side. The side that washed my feet. Read me the paper. Who saved that little girl. Loved by so many. But then there was the other side who hurt people. Hurt me. The cruel side. The withholding side. The wannabe Pimp.

"You're in the grip of a malevolent force. Go to the mountain."

Could there be truth to this? That one could be in a grip of a *malevolent f*orce? That he is? An energy -- a force -- a malevolent one, at that -- that has a hold of him? That had a hold on me? And kept me there, in spite of the pain? Like an addiction. It certainly felt that way.

That Flip Wilson was right? That there is a malevolent devil that actually made him do it? No joke. Could there be truth to this, crazy as that sounds? Are these forces the Archetypal energies that Jung wrote of? That can possess us. The energies warned of in Ephesians:

*For we wrestle not against flesh and blood, but against principalities, against powers,
against the rulers of the darkness of this world,
against spiritual wickedness in high places.*

Ephesians 6:12

Is it possible? That we battle not against people, but powers of the air? Wow. Powers that can take control of us? Grip us? Have us locked into their force?

Could that explain why a Senator will risk everything in a men's room in an airport somewhere in the Midwest? Or cause a hot, young Turk in Congress -- a darling of the Liberal Media, wed to an adored and great beauty, herself a Washington power player – to send photos and lurid texts to complete strangers, moving beyond provocative to pornographic just as he stands poised to possibly regain it all? Or a celebrity to crash and burn and claim he tried to stop 'whoring around' but was powerless against his desire for more? Why pornography, or drugs or alcohol will get out of control for so many? Literally ruining lives. Why a President who knows politically that the other side is gunning for him will foolishly enter a completely inappropriate relationship in the Oval Office? With a Jewish girl, no less. On her knees before him. Anyone say, Eve?

Or a Governor and Attorney General will destroy a career, opting for the alternate title of Client Number Nine, taken out just when we needed him the most.[90] A man who knew the perils of deregulation and derivatives. Who certainly could have warned, maybe even stepped in, and stopped it. Instead, he was stopped. Does it make it more interesting to learn that nine, as in Client No. 9, is the number of judgment? And not just his. All of ours. Does for me.

Or, on a more dangerous, albeit benign level, so many addicted to that smart gadget we carry around, that all began with the symbol of the bite of an apple. And the million other distractions that delight us, consume us. Keep us from our real purpose.

This is not to deny personal responsibility. We're always at choice. But is the "adversary" more nefarious – more powerful -- than we give him credit for? Does it truly travel the earth like a lion looking for prey to devour? With a purpose? Capturing our attention. Our affection. Beckoning.

Elliot... Bill... Tiger...

And beyond self-destruction, can this energy – this malevolent force --mesmerize not just a single individual, but a people, an entire nation?

No sooner had I had this thought, that I came across a book, *The Reluctant Prophet*, a record of dreams of an Orthodox Rabbi, originally self-published as a brochure under the title, "A Word of Warning". In the seventh dream,

---

[90] Who tried to warn of the Emperor with no clothes known as AIG, and sought to investigate, along with the other 50 State Attorney Generals, the subprime market, believing it be toxic, only to be stopped by the Bush Administration.

he saw a ferocious thunderstorm over his homeland of Romania, and from there a dark mass of clouds moving across Europe, beginning with Germany, then beyond. The meaning of the dream made known as he slept: That the virulent hatred of the Jews so prevalent at the time in Romania, was to, "make its rounds in other states, but will strike roots first in Germany, before it grips other countries."[91] The dream clearly foretold of the great darkness of the Holocaust that was to come, enveloping Europe, long before the First World War, the resulting destruction and poverty, the grueling Depression, the rise of Fascism – factors often cited, if not to justify, then to attempt to understand how such evil could take hold. In fact, this *word of warning* was published in 1881, when Jewish communities across Europe were untouched and thriving.

But what interested me more, beyond the prophecy, is this idea of energies... malevolent forces... like the darkness in the dream... that can grab hold of an entire population or large segments. As the beautiful Bulgarian girl in *Casablanca* pleads to Rick, *"Things are very bad there, Monsieur. A devil has the People by the throat."* Could that really be? That a force, an energy, as in that dream, can mesmerize. Rally it to its evil cause? Is that what happened then? Or in Rwanda? Bosnia? East Timor? The Sudan? The Congo? ISIS?

Is that what's happening now? In the violence that we witness every day in all its hideous forms, from Syria to Iraq, to Sandy Hook, San Bernardino, Orlando, Nice, Chicago, Cleveland, and on and on. The list grows by the day. Can this explain how the lone wolf can be radicalized to murder innocent children, colleagues, countrymen and

---

[91] Kirsch, James, "The Reluctant Prophet", (Sherbourne Press, Inc., 1973), p.55.

friends? And, why, more often than not, those nearest and dearest, exclaim in alarm, that's not my child. My child couldn't do this.

Or, in the greed that's sweeping the world? Fifty Thousand factories move out of America and a Republican Presidential hopeful proclaims "It's your own fault!" to the 20 million left jobless in the wreckage of outsourcing, offshoring and "free" trade, let alone, the crash of '08. The callous disregard for those left behind is shocking. "Let him die!" a Tea Party advocate yells out, addressing the plight of the uninsured, and those same hopefuls on the stage, to the man, and woman, remain silent. Is this America? The party that prides itself on Christian values? Withholding unemployment benefits to those on the precipice, until further tax cuts for the rich are appropriated? At Christmas? Eliminating essential programs, healthcare that literally keeps people alive, all in the name of fiscal responsibility, while heaping more and more on those who don't need it, including themselves. All the while decrying the death of God in the public square, and the resulting waning of America? A "populist" takes office, and his very first act eliminating a mortgage relief program designed for the same people he claimed to save. The hypocrisy is dizzying.

"In their greed, the new Pharisees."

I hear this on waking one morning. For those of you unfamiliar with the term, as I certainly was, the Pharisees were the *Uber* religious, I came to discover, the ultra-faithful, the most devout, prayed the loudest, tithed the most generously, but with the coldest hearts. Who engineered and insisted on the death of Jesus. Could this greed and those working tirelessly in pursuit of it, in support of it, on whatever side of the aisle, whatever political party, in whatever industry, or stripe, wherever in the World, indeed be the new Pharisees? Only this time the Christ they seek to destroy is not Jesus himself, but, as Jesus warned, the Christ of Matthew 25:

Then he will say to those on his left, 'Depart from me, you who are cursed, into the eternal fire prepared for the devil and his angels. For I was hungry and you gave me nothing to eat, I was thirsty and you gave me nothing to drink, I was a stranger and you did not invite me in, I needed clothes and you did not clothe me, I was sick and in prison and you did not look after me.'
They also will answer, 'Lord, when did we see you hungry or thirsty or a stranger or needing clothes or sick or in prison, and did not help you?'
He will reply, 'Truly I tell you, whatever you did not do for one of the least of these, you did not do for me.'

Matthew 25:41-45

Or, the Christ within themselves.

"You're in the grip of a malevolent force. Go to the mountain."

It's easy to judge. Much harder to remember that everyone in the story, this story, our story, the good and the bad, the villain and the hero/heroine, is in service to this greater Divine pattern. That we're all in this together, playing a role. That each of us is made in the image and likeness of God. All finding our way back to God. Individually and collectively.

But there's a point in time that one must become conscious of what role he or she is playing. And what journey he or she is on. And to recognize that the ultimate challenge of this journey is to break free of that malevolent force. Whether the betrayed or the betrayer. To do the work. To take the journey. To answer the call. To go to the wilderness, like the woman. And know the Truth with a capital "T" which is God. And like the betrayed, hang out with it. Become intimate with it. Lie with it. Seek it. And in that atmosphere, those ethers, die to yourself. And break free of this force that's got a hold of you, driving you to your own destruction.

"Come out from amongst thee!"

I hear one morning in meditation. I was caught in the story of the world on that particular day, railing against the contentiousness and greed and partisanship and gridlock that is our government. And when I went into meditation, I heard those words and knew they were biblical. I assumed what was meant by them was to separate oneself from the crowd, the masses. That the path is narrow, I've come to understand. That one must turn away from the world. Come out from it.

And, in fact, the passage in Corinthians says as much.[92] But what I heard that day, was immediately followed by this:

"See the story from a higher level. Go higher."

Beyond the story. Beyond Politics. Contentiousness. Winning. Go higher. Above the story. The anger. The fear. Greed is not your nature. Love is. God is. Compassion is. That's who you are. Who we all are. Be careful. One's heart can harden in rarefied atmospheres. The ego is a demanding master. And God warns that he will remove himself at some point and it will be impossible for some to understand or even hear the truth. That this grip on their very being, their thoughts, their behavior will be fixed.

Jesus was very specific to what happens to those not ready when he returns, or to those who have squandered their opportunity on earth, given the power he tells us we have. Not to accumulate wealth. Not to be good stewards in that sense. But to be good stewards of the power of the Holy Spirit, that is in each of us. Available to all. To do as he has, and so much more. To move that mountain. Having instructed us through his teaching how to access that power.

The lamp light of the virgins of Matthew 25 is the light within. *Ignite it.* "Let thine eye be single and the body shall

---

[92] 2 Corinthians 6:17 "Wherefore come out from among them, and be ye separate saith the Lord, and touch not the unclean thing; and I will receive you."

be full of light."[93] Yes, single-minded purpose of seeking God[94], but I also believe the single eye is the third eye. *Open it* in meditation. And love and light will pour in. Jesus went to the desert for forty days and meditated. Meditation, that at least for me, along with reading the Word of God, *purifies* in its vibration. Literally to be washed in the Word. In the blood. Once again, these are not just words. It's an experience. You will feel it. To balance all parts of you as represented by the Cross. Jesus was perfectly balanced. Male, Female, Logical, Intuitive, Spirit, and Man. The Hindus have their mudras. The Catholics and Christians the motion of the cross, that to me, is the armor of God. Try it. It all has a vibration. That *Heals*. Tap into it. Bring magic to your life. No waiting for the next world. A better one, that awaits you here, in fact, is calling you. Right now.

Go to your wilderness, wherever that is, close your eyes, and say 'I'm here." "I'm ready." "I'm listening." And do it every day. Throughout the day. Even just for a moment. Close your eyes and turn your attention to God. And open your heart. And feel it ignite within you. Wash over you. And your dreams will sweeten. And your life will sweeten. Especially in these tumultuous times, when your joy is being robbed, and your temperature is rising moment by moment, do it. Wake up!!

You have the ability to break free, to go higher, to walk in this vibration – the vibration of God -- with an open heart, and an enthusiasm for life, for each day, for the beauty of it –

---

[93] Matthew 6:22
[94] Next time you feel anxious, close your eyes and turn your attention to God—actually say those words, declare it – and see what happens, as the anxiety disappears and a peace that defies understanding moves in. It's magic.

the adventure of it – the joy of it -- in this world right now, no matter what the circumstance. With a love for all around you, infused with Spirit, you just can't help it. To anchor heaven on earth right now. To live there, right now. To know God, most of all, right now. And all else shall be added. I only wish I had known about this earlier, had tapped into it earlier. To have walked in the world this way. A world that is enchanted. Rich. Endlessly interesting. You can't beat it.

"Wanna' hang out with me? More than anything?"

I believe, as with me, God is asking each of you.

Whatever else you choose to do, seek the Kingdom, first thing, every day, for the joy it will bring you, the enthusiasm for life, and, finally, frankly, if there is a New World coming, – a New Jerusalem – if we really are in the last chapter of this great story, he only wants people who can answer "yes" to that question. Can you blame him? Only those who have taken the time – the steps -- to get ready. To make the necessary preparations, to open their hearts. To ignite the light within them. To kick up the waters – the living waters -- within you. To wash away the grit of the journey. Restore the years the locusts have eaten. *"I make all things new,"* he said. These are not just words. You will experience it, in yourself. See it with your own eyes.

"When you left all the magic did,"

Jack said to me. It was gratifying to hear. The girl in me glowed. But it wasn't me. It was the God in me. The vibration in me. The conversations. The Word of God. The dreams. His soul was being fed. Lifted. And we were being blessed. And, yes, it was magic.

Now it's his job to do the work. To walk with God, hang out with God. To look away, turn away from this world. Moses took the people to the edge of the Promised Land, but he couldn't take them in. Only Joshua/Jeshua could. And only after he slew the enemy, destroyed the city, and rescued a whore turned spy. We, each of us, have this journey to make, within ourselves. Someone may take you to the edge of the Promised Land, some reading, some preacher, some rabbi, some Iman, but at some point, stepping fully into it is your work, alone. Ultimately, the path *is* narrow. Room for one. Nothing, however, more complicated than hanging out with God. Reading what inspires. Closing your eyes. Feeling the presence within you. Activating it. Letting it love you. Letting it heal you. And ultimately, transform you.

The parables are about getting ready. The Sermon on the Mount is about getting ready. Revelation is the final journey. The final chapter. The final choice.

The Spirit and the bride say, "Come!" And let him who hears say, "Come!" Whoever is thirsty, let him come; and whoever wishes, let him take the free gift of the water of life.

Revelation 22:17

Blessed are those who wash their robes, that they may have the right to the tree of life and may go through the gates into the city.

Revelation 22:14

Begin that process. Purify. "Wash your robes." Ignite the light within you.

"You're in the grip of a malevolent force. Go to the mountain."

For the mountain, in The Bible, is God.

In the dream, Jack did. He flew to that mountain, was lifted up, above the danger, and survived.

But in life, at least at that moment, he refused.

Too much fun in the grip.

He dreams he's at a party in Hollywood – he's a regular, he confides, some kind of party circuit. In the dream, he's standing on a hillside, great view of the city -- two women in the background – when suddenly he hears the voice of a man. It appears the man is really disappointed. He's offered Jack a job, to work for him. Speak for him at corporate events. Represent him. Jack tells the Man he doesn't know a thing about his business, or what he's selling. He wouldn't know what to say. He's sure to fail. Bad for Jack. Bad for the Man. Bad for business. The Man assures him he'll tell him what to say, give him the words. Jack's not entirely convinced he can pull it off, but mulls over the offer. But before making a decision, or perhaps to avoid it, he concludes there's no way he can get home, pack, and get to LAX for the flight the man's booked for him. It leaves at 6. It's already 3. No way he'll make it. Not from where he is. At this party in the Hollywood Hills.

No sooner does he have this thought, then a spaceship appears on the horizon, a UFO, headed right at him. There's no escaping it. It draws close, hovering, only inches away. Suddenly, abruptly, a piercing prism of light scans him from head to toe. And at that moment in the dream, he had the feeling that he'd betrayed the Man with the offer. That he'd given away all his secrets – The Man's secrets -- to the Alien. Everything he'd been taught, shown, handed over to the enemy.

Chapter 17

Thirty minutes of Silence

I begin to warn people.
"I may be crazy, but if I'm not,
all hell's gonna break loose at the end of July 2008."
July came. The month was quiet. Nothing extraordinary. Then,
at the end of August, Lehman began to unravel, and the world
economies stood at the precipice.

"You're a month off."

That's all he says. Almost chiding. Smug. Pleased. Obama's in office by the time we meet again, and the Market's in free fall. I couldn't resist seeing him. Too much is going on in the world. And we share this story that to me is so clearly unfolding. But it's been a while since we've met, and he's cold, detached -- to me, the story, everything.

I'd only seen him a couple times since I'd walked away for Rio and chosen God. I'd sneak in a birthday or a Christmas, occasionally. But for the most part, as hard as it was, I'd stayed away. Stuck to it. Kept my promise. This time, it had been at least a year or more.

The last time we met, I'd given him a belated birthday gift that I'd been carrying around for months. A prism of clear crystal, naturally divided into four quadrants. Something like this:

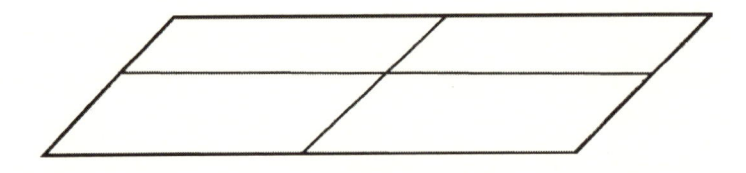

It reminded me so much of him. The two upper quadrants, the "higher" Self, smaller than the lower. Unless, of course, you flipped it over, in which case the higher outweighed the lower. That's how he was. One minute one way. The next minute, the other.

He smiled on seeing me that night, in a way I'd never seen him smile. Full out. Unabashed. No holds barred. But unfortunately, I'd seen him briefly the day before. He informed me then, that he and the Cuban girl had split. She got tired of waiting for him. As he put it, his expiration date was up, about a year before. He remembered the exact day. It was clear he wasn't over her. And if he missed anyone, it hadn't been me. And was still looking to get out of town. No more Cuba. Now it was Puerto Rico, South America, New Orleans, maybe Mexico, wherever. So, when he smiled at me that following night, so happy to see me, that I was there, I didn't smile back. I held any feelings I had in check. I was just nervous. And tired of this. Shut down.

As we sat and talked, about life, his art, my writing, he toyed with the crystal, turning it over and over in his hand. His behavior otherwise passive, glued to the chair. Nothing had changed. He was remote as ever. Maybe if I had met his smile.

At some point, his ex-wife came in unexpectedly and burst into tears on seeing me, conveying in her outburst that my being there was somehow good for him. Maybe he's not as great as he says, I wonder. The evening wore on, pleasant, but not much more. He invites me to join him for dinner. I pass, and he walks me to my car, carrying a piece of art that he's given me for my new place. That will be perfect. That I love. Truth is I kind of weaseled it out of him. I gave him the crystal, he gave me the art. Not a bad deal. The night is not a total waste. He tries to engage me on the way to my car, and kiss me when we get there. I don't respond. Just a quick peck and I'm gone. But as I drive away, I am overwhelmed by a feeling of love for him that washes over me. I want to turn back, to go back, and tell him. But I don't. It'll just be awkward, and I keep driving. I write him the next day, something about seeing him, how lovely it was, how great the art looks, that I love it, and he writes back and tells me how much he loves the crystal. A small flurry of emails over the next few days, then nothing. Except an all too familiar pain. And I know I'm right. That I've got to let go. For good. I do it in meditation, as much as I don't want to. "Take him from me," I say. "Take this pain." Before I go to sleep that night, I think of him longingly, and force myself to let go once more. One more time. One last time.

The next day I stay away. It's not easy. It's like I've gotten hooked back into his energy. That string that connects us. But I stay away. And on the dot of three, just as David and Rio are returning home, I get an email from him. *"You're gonna like this,"* the subject line reads. It seems he's been sleeping with the crystal under his head since he saw me, and the prior night he writes, he dreamt that two sets of hearts left the crystal, a large set of hearts, and a small set. Remember the Quadrants? In the Crystal? The larger two and the smaller two? The Higher and the lower? The hearts-- the love of the Higher Self in us -- and the love of the lower self. He wondered in the dream as he watched the hearts float away, how something so smooth and so round could live in that block of crystal. And when he awoke, the crystal under his head had broken in half. Literally.

I had let go of the love in meditation, and before I went to bed, and he dreamt of the love, the hearts, leaving the crystal, the large and the small, the higher and the lower, and beneath his head, the crystal snapped in half.

We were done. Maybe I had manifested it by letting go. Or maybe, just maybe, I heard the voice of God in all this saying,

"Enough you two."

"You're a month off."

When I said all hell was to break loose, it was because the book of Revelations talks in terms of a seven-year cycle, and while I thought the seven years began with the dream and Katrina, in meditation, months later, it came through clearly that the seven years began with the tsunami in Indonesia, eight months earlier. I remembered thinking in the aftermath of that terrible tragedy, how strange it was that something so apocalyptic would occur the day after Christmas. Only years later would I realize the profound implication: Based on that event, the seven-year period of Revelation would end on Christmas Day -- the mass coming of the Christ consciousness – Christ mass.

Three and a half years from the tsunami, the mid- point, the beginning of what is called the Great Tribulation, put us at the end of July 2008. Ergo, if I was right, all hell was to break loose about then. Half way through.

We're in the alley, fresh from the beach. Jack's rinsing off Max.
"How are you, Jack?" Rodriguez, the short-order cook from next door calls out.
"How could I not be good?" Jack replies, "I'm washing Judy's feet."

Those days were long gone. But, surely he had to see. My buddy.

So, I was thirty days off. Big deal. It's not like it was six months. Or a year. I tried to make light of it, but inside I agreed. It was a big deal. Either it was game on, or the timing of the Katrina dream was, in fact, just coincidence. And in true game mode, thirty days doesn't cut it. That is, until I got into the car, flipped on the radio and heard this:

> *And when he had opened the seventh seal, there was silence in heaven about the space of half an hour*
>
> **Revelation 8:1**

Huh? And then a day later, I heard it again. Different station. Different preacher. Heck, I didn't even know the Bible talked in terms of a half an hour.

Thirty minutes of silence, of prayer for the inhabitants of the earth, or perhaps, as some suggest, the calm before the storm.

Thirty minutes. Thirty days. Not a big stretch. Was the period from late July to late August that calm? For, thirty days later, that hell I warned about breaking loose, did just that, as markets and lives crashed.

But Christmas 2011, the end of the seven years, came and went without incident. Unremarkable, at least to the human eye. And certainly, the tragic and catastrophic events one associates with Revelation had in no way come to pass, by any definition. And I began to wonder if I was wrong about all this. Yes, the individual soul's journey is the story of the Bible, is indeed the journey back to Eden, but the collective? The idea that we may be living through this now, together? Am I wrong? I see this story everywhere, but am I wrong? What am I missing?

What I'm missing is that at the end of Revelation, a wedding has occurred. The wedding. And the bride is presented. That thought drops into my head as I'm walking on the beach, in early 2012 from out of nowhere.

In ancient Jewish times, I come to find out, when this story was written, Jewish weddings would begin with an agreement made between the bridegroom and the father of the bride. A price for her would be established and paid by the groom. A marriage covenant was drawn up and signed. A glass of wine shared with the bride. For all intents and purposes, the two were married. This was the ceremony. That was it. The agreement could only be rescinded by a decree of divorce. Once the deal was set and sealed, the bridegroom would depart to prepare a place for her, a home for them, typically an extension of his father's house. He would return for her upon its completion – a year or so later – usually at night, unannounced, to take her back. To take her home. Word would travel ahead of him along the route, of the groom's pending arrival, for the bride to make herself ready. Once collected, the two journeyed back to his father's house, and upon arriving, would spend the next seven days in seclusion in the bridal chamber.

Meals were left at the door. No one would see them. For seven days, a time just for them. No TV. No cell phones, Internet, newspapers. No new friends met at the Tiki bar. No. Just a bed. Great food. And someone you love. The ultimate honeymoon. And only after seven days was the door to the chamber opened. Did the couple emerge. The groom presenting the bride, and the two welcoming everyone to the party, known back then as the wedding feast.

There's much in that description that has direct parallels to the teachings of Jesus. "I prepare a place for you." "My father's house has many mansions." "No one knows the time of my coming." And surely, the presentation of the bride at the end of Revelation. And the wedding feast.

I've come to believe that this seven-day period translates to an additional seven years, making it from beginning to end a fourteen-year story, in which the events of the tribulation continue to build and climax. [95] And only those ready to attend the wedding – the virgins with sufficient oil in their lamps – the guests, purified, dressed in the appropriate garment, the white linen of the saints, will gain admission. Many of the parables told by Jesus were warnings. But few as clear as the Parable of the Wedding Feast. The garment symbolic of our consciousness, purified through meditation and prayer and just hanging out with God. You see, we're all invited to this Wedding Feast. But whether we opt to go, or are ready to attend, well, that's up to us. Many are called but few are chosen – make that, ready.

"The kingdom of heaven is like a king who prepared a wedding banquet for his son.
He sent his servants to those who had been invited to the banquet to tell them to come, but they refused to come.
"Then he sent some more servants and said, 'Tell those who have been invited that I have prepared my dinner: My oxen and fattened cattle have been butchered, and everything is ready. Come to the wedding banquet.'

---

[95] Mirroring the fourteen years that Jacob worked for Rachel and Leah. Remember, Jacob is Eve. This is her story of redemption. Seven years for Adam. And seven years for Lucifer.

"But they paid no attention and went off—one to his field, another to his business. The rest seized his servants, mistreated them and killed them. The king was enraged. He sent his army and destroyed those murderers and burned their city.

"Then he said to his servants, 'The wedding banquet is ready, but those I invited did not deserve to come. So go to the street corners and invite to the banquet anyone you find.' So the servants went out into the streets and gathered all the people they could find, the bad as well as the good, and the wedding hall was filled with guests.

"But when the king came in to see the guests, he noticed a man there who was not wearing wedding clothes. He asked, 'How did you get in here without wedding clothes, friend?' The man was speechless.

"Then the king told the attendants, 'Tie him hand and foot, and throw him outside, into the darkness, where there will be weeping and gnashing of teeth.'

"For many are invited, but few are chosen."

Matthew 22:1-14

This is the work of this moment, I believe. To make oneself ready. To meditate. To pray. To seek the face of God. In the silence. To purify in that vibration. This is our mission. And, perhaps it always was. But it certainly, I believe, is calling us right now.

The world has seen hard times before, I know. As bad as this, worse than this. If it wasn't for the dream and Katrina - its meaning and its timing - my warning that all hell was about to break loose at the end of July 2008, and the crash coming on its heels –and lastly, the prophetic dream of 9/11, I wouldn't be saying any of this. I may not know the exact time all this will play out, but is it all really, meaningless coincidence?

Oh, and one more reason:

> "So many traitors and so many fiends
> We're being worn out like a pile of jeans
> Holy cow, we might have to throw in the towel
> It's like a finale and it's time to take a bow
> What are we gonna do now?
> Liberate for goodness sake!
> Why would you wait when the world's at stake?!"
> Rio Wyles "We Will Prevail"

Yes, that Rio. The very same one. My son. The boy who struggled to make sense.

The rapper, now known as Soulshocka.

> "On the employment line, you're annoyed this time
> Finally, at the counter, all you get is a fine
> Nothing but swine stealing dimes wasting other people's time
> And you're trying to survive with the other 99
> You're McDivin
> They're high fivin
> What's with the creation of this frustration?
> It's a re-evaluation
> Turn the radio, change the station!
> It's a game of Truth or Dare

The rich don't seem to care
What seems unfair is fair.
Prepare!
There's a mission that you're dissin
And if you're talkin' you can't listen.
Shhhhhh......![96]

Be still and know that I am God.
Psalm 46:10

"In any great story, the villain appears half way through,"
Jack called out that final day, as I walked away.
"He has."
I turned back
Our eyes met, mine knowing, his searching.
I smiled, giving him a look.
"Ah, come on...."

---

[96] "We Will Prevail", R. Wyles

Chapter 18

The Final Chapter

As you can see, Rio's doing great. Amazing actually. Miraculous. Even David can't believe it. Can't explain it. Is delighted by it. Enchanted by it. Yes, everyday life can still be a struggle for Rio in the simplest of ways, but on most days, our conversations are as sophisticated and natural as any I have. Both as to language and content. But on others, or with strangers, the most obvious word will elude him.

As to his lyrics, that's a whole other story. They come from another place. He doesn't talk that way. He doesn't even think that way, in his beliefs – dismisses most of what I say as totally bonkers. And, certainly not on that level. Few do. And doesn't understand the meaning of what he's written. Yet, he's warning us. Of something that's coming, and what we need to do.

He's also talking to the darkness in many of his raps. And saying in no uncertain terms, you're done. It's over.

I've gone back and forth about my own warnings in this book. Rio's words are a good part of the reason I kept them in. Unlike me, his words for the most part, do not come from the cognitive, left brain, or observation, or research. Rather, they arise from the intuitive part of his brain. He goes into the silence and catches it. Works with it. This is not to minimize his own genius. He just happens to collaborate with the best that there is. The Highest in him. The God in him. In that high vibration. And what he gets in Rap, its language, its symbols, its message, is like second nature to me, as a result of my own dreams, my own journey, and the resultant work to understand it all. Like I once said, we're in this together. Partners in Crime.

Living with Rio, being on this journey, has been beyond my wildest dreams, and you know, I've had some pretty wild ones. Going from witnessing his struggle, the heartbreak of it, to seeing him confident, killing it on stage at Carnegie Hall, the United Nations, the Pantages – surely the stuff of dreams. Certainly, of answered prayer. Lightyears away from that scene outside of Barnes & Noble, when I cried for his life, and mine. It's a bloody miracle, courtesy of God. And what's great about miracles, is you not only get to witness and celebrate the result, which is mind-boggling all by its lonesome, but it also comes with the added bonus of being in the Presence every time you witness it. Every time he performs. Every time he uses a phrase that floors me. Writes a lyric. Makes an observation. Has an abstract thought. Every time life feels normal.

And well beyond all the luminaries he's performed with, the red carpet, and the adulation, and even his mind-blowing artistry, most of all, for me, it's what he's saying. Above all else. To be privy to that wisdom. For me, that's the gift. I've attached his work in the Appendix, not to sit in wonder – definitely do that—it is nothing short of that miracle -- but for its content. Read what he's saying. What he's trying to get us to hear.

And finally, the gift of knowing him. He's gotta be the loveliest human being. Not a drop of ego. Just a truly great person. Sweet as they come. One day in complete exasperation of trying to teach him something for the thousandth time, I blurted out in frustration, "What am I gonna do with you?" And without a moment's hesitation, he answered, "Just love me, Mom."

Great lesson. For all of us.

But regardless of my warnings and dreams, or Rio's words, don't come to this work out of fear. Come for the love and the wisdom and a way of walking in the world that's like nothing else. Come for the joy you'll feel for no reason. The happiness. The sweetness. A refreshing shower for the heart, the body, and the soul. And, come for the magic.

"Yes, magic is real,"

I wanted to scream out to the young man in *Boyhood* when he asked his father if magic was real. It broke my heart to hear his answer. Magic is real. Ours to have. Our lives are enchanted. If you see it. If you tap into it. If you're open to it. The Universe is always talking to you. You just gotta' listen.

"As you look back over your life, it can seem
to have had a plot,
as though composed by a novelist."
Arthur Schopenhauer

We each have our own tale. Equally enchanting as anything I've experienced. As anything I've written here. Or more so. Start seeking it. Begin the work. Find your wilderness. Take the journey.

I'm still on it, happily, trying not to fall off, to wander, to be distracted. It's so easy. There's so much to grab our attention. The politics and the story --- especially the story. It's like a movie playing out right in front of us. The world our screen. And what a story! Right out of Le Carre.

Let alone our personal stories, our marriages, our families and friends, careers, technology, Facebook, Twitter, finances...so many ways to get lost. To be distracted. Iyanla Vanzant once remarked that the real WMD's, weapons of mass destruction, lay between our two ears. What we think about. All the negativity and negative self-talk. I'd add to that weapons of mass distraction.

But, don't let it. Begin to see it all from a higher level. The message it has for you. For all of us. The purpose it serves.

> *Globalization really smashed and hit the nation.*
> *In heavy rotation.*
> *Like dominoes falling*
> *It's a calling....*[97]

Hear that. What he's saying. It's a calling.

Answer the call. Find your sacred wilderness, wherever that is. Begin the work. Seek the Kingdom. Every day. Cry

---

[97] Ibid., We Will Prevail

out the pain accumulated over the years, from whatever heartbreak or disappointment with life, or betrayal. Blow out the rage of pent- up anger. And anger over this moment. Then, close your eyes, and breathe in love. And breathe out peace. And breathe in love again. And breathe out peace. And let that breath wash over you. And feel it. Let it envelop you. Let it transform you. Let it heal you.

For I believe that is its purpose.

To know God.

Nothing less.

Bon Voyage!!!
From the Wilderness
With love,
Judith

Epilogue

Infinity And the Mystery of Mind

I was alone that night
a giant amber moon
was hanging low
upon a silent ocean
the velvet sky
of midnight blue was lined
with mystic brilliance

star-spangled...

timeless beauty incarnate...

I couldn't help
but look towards
the vastness of it all

the Milky Way and its Infinity...

could anybody ever comprehend
the all-encompassing
never ending

Finality of Infinity?

I tried to focus on a spot
beyond the line of stars
and failed miserably

I became hopelessly overwhelmed
by the vastness of it all

and then I saw a shooting star

following with my eyes

its downward path

I realised

*that this was really not
Infinity at all...*

Infinity carries on...

and on beyond the stars...

and never ends...

*this Galaxy is but
a tiny part of it...*

*and suddenly the giant moon
seemed nothing but a tiny speck
within the outstretched
velvet depth of vacuum
filled with stars*

*against the mystic,
darkness permeated,
stretches of the wide expanse
it faded into non-existence...*

And then I understood Infinity

*but realised
that I could never
comprehend the*

Mystery of Mind

...at all...

*for however vast the Universe
it snugly fits within
the confines of my thoughts...*

a miracle...

God's vast creation...

in a nutshell...

*and never forgotten,
the beauty of the amber moon
still glows within my mind
and I just need to think to be there
on that night
in the presence of that
mystic vision*

*to see that moon
and never be alone again...*

© *Antoinette LeRoux*

With permission

To be continued…

"Comin to the Wedding like a ringer

Mr. Rap Singer"

Appendix I
The Lyrics of Rio Wyles

Soulshocka

Kick in the Door remix
Track by DJ Premier
Lyrics by Rio Wyles

Shocka!

Salutations
Sending out the invitations
Let's get ready for the celebration
Got 'em patiently waiting debating and contemplating
If you're participating in hating homie you're fading
Got em ready for battle. Got em shakin, like a rattle,
Skeedaddle
Bullets streaming down like a paddle
shmucks shoveling crap manure like cattle
climbing to the top of the castle with no hassle
you rascal

Comin through swingin
this is what I'm bringin
Ringa ding dingin hear the telephone ringin
It ain't close to call till the fat lady singin
Don't come back Jack
I'll be thinkin when your sinkin

Hook
Kick in the door gotta keep it hardcore

Like you never heard this before
Kick in the door gotta keep it hardcore
Shine so bright till I make your eye sore

Repeat

Verse 2

Its the Mr. Hussle. Tussle with the muscle
In the threshold have to be old or you fold
Out here in the cold to the troll's middle finger
Comin to the wedding like the ringer Mr. rap singer
Slinger to the clinger may the last resort
Then we put em in the fort till it's time to report
and take em to court
See I take my life with strife hard like a knife,
Go riding like a bike, take a hike what's wrong is right,
I make the present like a gift and open it
take the hole and poke in it
have a smoke and toke in it,
choke on it, put a rope on it,
I might make you croak on it, shit

Verse 3

See I'm getting there accordingly, why are reporting me,
Extorting me, distorting me? Got my warranties,
If I can get there right where I can afford to be
Man, time flashes into ashes
passes in the masses, like an infection itches with the rashes
Life's outta control like the system and it crashes

Too much commotion it hatches
Decomposes it trashes
Right in front of your eyelashes
And it's hard to concentrate, re-evaluate fate mate
you wanna take the fish on the bait and participate,
open up the gate and relate? Great!
But if not shut your mouth better mute it, Stupid.

Malfunction

Produced by Joe Seabe
Lyrics by Rio Wyles

This is for you
You know who you are

mal, mal, mal, mal, mal, mal, mal, mal
malfunction

I rip the jacka'
hold it so close like a mappa'
come too close and I could crack up
I'm not on a path I'm on a tracka'
where you at, huh?

see everybody yeah they want to be famous
but one day they'll still all forget what the hell your name is
but i can't take this
make this the greatest
one day people might look at you like your faceless
you're not a Lutheran but you're a saintist
holding on but you might be weightless
people think you're old school
when you thinkin you're the latest
can't forsake this
Think you can relate to this?

Malfunction
bout to be clutching
from all the pain and touching
there's nothing left
keep it all in check
malfunction
some people turn away
but I gotta say, Uh
malfunction
it's crazy, huh?
Feelin' like you're about to be scarred
and can't say that you are,
you can't save it, huh?
you can't play it, huh?
malfunction
even if they don't' know who you are
malfunction

Now your life is upside down
quit coming around
with that jibber jabber sound
feelin like a letdown
now you're being tracked down
wondering where it's at now
hoping you come back now
with all that commotion
under a spell from a potion
quit complaining start explaining
it's like a drama case
and now you're fainting

wondering why you came out of this place
it's all a waste
a big disgrace
hoping people will say welcome back like Mase
joining in the human race
feelin' like life is an apple
and you want to take a taste
no one wants to see your face
sayin that you're perfect
sayin you don't deserve it
it aint' worth it
jerking it but you're working it
see you're on a trail raining hail
Nothing you know will prevail

malfunction
bout to be clutching
from all the pain and touching
there's nothing left
keep it all in check
malfunction
some people turn away
but I gotta say, uh
malfunction
it's crazy, huh?
feelin like you're about to be scarred
and can't say that you are
you can't save it, huh? you can't play it, huh?
malfunction
even if they don't' know who you are

malfunction

stop
wait a minute
can't see what you're getting
you don't know where you're heading
quit forgetting
I'm done with your snitching
quit bitching
tellin tales on a brother
doin it like no other
feelin everybody's gonna get you undercover
you don't know who to turn to a friend or a lover
you're a sick suckka
mean mugga'
perverted thugger
quit snitching
now you're headed out on a mission
with no condition
in the zone is where you're hitching
wishing you had a choice between life and death
that's what you're missing
now you're giving me that sensitive act
I don't play that
thinking you're a straight cat
talking riffraff with that crap
somebody taps you on your shoulder
next thing you know your whole life is over
you're about to be terminalized
with no surprise

you're about to apologize
you're about to recognize
what's ahead of you when you open your eyes

malfunction
bout to be clutching
from all the pain and touching
there's nothing left
keep it all in check
malfunction
some people turn away
but I gotta say, uh
malfunction
it's crazy, huh?
feelin like you're about to be scarred
and can't say that you are (you can't save it, huh? you can't play it, huh?)
malfunction
even if people don't' know who you are
malfunction

Bonus tracks
it's a meltdown
it's not where it started
people out there being dearly departed
you know it's not heaven, it's heck now
now you're out there freezing
but it's a hundred degreezin
it's treason
give me a reason or a revelation

maybe all you need is some meditation
it's not an obligation, it's a celebration
listening to the sounds of the Rhythm Nation
no hesitation or surprise
now you open your eyes
and realize
now you look inside
now that you hold your pride
you have your mouth open wide
stuck somewhere between having a cat there
or being tongue-tied
in a fire being fried
the obligation is next
and the quest begins after sunrise

see it's like a puzzle and it's a natural fitting
you thinking I'm kidding?
you're on a time machine, sitting
stuck in between
on to the next scene
you're in a super hero movie
and you're the fiend
a mass murderer, serial killer
starring in the remix of the remake of Michael Jackson's
thrilla
a drug deala'
stacking up coins like a milla
pounding your chest like king kong the gorilla
thinking you're shot calling
thinking you're Jim Jones and you're balling

nothing but stalling
from falling
cause I'm the bone crusher
the original structure
nobody can help you now
not any way
not any how
out in the cold on a mountain
thirty feet deep below
in an avalanche
and you're holdin on to nothin' but a thin branch
hoping you'll manage
hoping you won't die
hoping it's a lie
that a small population will cry
so say your prayers
if you dare
beware
the end is nare
treading on the path
you'll feel the wrath
the power
It's a nuclear shower
on the top of the tower
feel it going down
it might be sweet
it might be sour
then it overloads
then starts to explode
at the end of the round

it will start to countdown
uh

malfunction
bout to be clutching
from all the pain and touching
there's nothing left
keep it all in check
malfunction
some people turn away
but I gotta say, uh
malfunction
it's crazy, huh?
feelin like you're about to be scarred
and can't say that you are (you can't save it, huh? you can't play it, huh?)
malfunction
even if people don't' know who you are
malfunction
5-4-3-2-1
Malfunction

It's Shocking

Lyrics by Rio Wyles
Beat by August McAdoo

INTRO

So you want to know how I got my name?

Do you want to know what it is, why it is, why my name is Soulshocka?

Alright, I'll tell ya

Hook

it's shocking, how I rhyme this way
it's shocking, who I was and who I am today
it's shocking, I might mock ya
who am I? I'm Soulshocka

it's shocking, how I rhyme this way
it's shocking, who I was and who I am today
it's shocking, poppin up like Orville Redenbocka
who am I? I'm Soulshocka

Verse 1

Comin in or out.
scream or better shout
man watch your mouth
know what I'm talking about
Have any doubt? go ahead and pout'

watch out!
In the middle of a drought
feel that time is running out
Get suspicious
gotch ya swimming with the fishes
very vicious
Say your prayers and your wishes
I'm about to end up clocking
Do you hear the beat walking?
right behind you and it's stalking?
and it's mocking?
So you want to know my name?
its shocking!
Wanna know the game?
nothin but a barker hawking
Chasin a fame that's hard to maintain
in vain
what a pain
bout to go crazy down the drain
insane in the brain hot like a flame
when I step on it, it won't be the same.
It's very well plain
how I get my name
So right here before us
Here comes the chorus

Hook

it's shocking, how I rhyme this way
it's shocking, who I was and who I am today
it's shocking, I might mock ya

who am I? I'm Soulshocka

it's shocking, how I rhyme this way
it's shocking, who I was and who I am today
it's shocking, poppin up like Orville Redenbocka
who am I? I'm Soulshocka

Verse 2

Can't stand the anxiety deep inside of me
And my conscience saying why are you lying to me?
How bout them motor skills that don't pay the bills?
Make a life from this strife.
Don't that give you chills?
This game is my salvation.
Get it with no hesitation
Gotta get decent exposure, keep my composure
Keep my head up like a soldier
But the isolation drivin me crazy!
So I'm cutting corners, having boulders on my shoulders!
On the cliff on the edge like folders
But I'm not foldin I'm holdin
So, move over it's about to get colder
It ain't over till I say it's over!
Knick knack paddy wack rat a tat tat
Bout to bring it right back as a matter of fact
So listen up unless you want to get jacked
Cause I'm on the mat up to bat
How do you like that?!

Hook

it's shocking, how I rhyme this way
it's shocking, who I was and who I am today
it's shocking, I might mock ya
who am I? I'm Soulshocka
it's shocking, how I rhyme this way
it's shocking, who I was and who I am today
it's shocking, poppin up like Orville Redenbocka
who am I? I'm Soulshocka

Verse 3

It's shocking how I flow
The diabolical, there he go, there he go
Watch him spit ah sh**
Like you don't know?
That I put in the work
to put me center of attention
Did I forget to mention?
Bout to go out and
gotta get my henchmen
I'm on a roll
Someone said, damn you got soul
I'm just reaching my goal
you know
Bout to break the mold it's plain to see
It's a guarantee
Who's gonna bring it to the max?
Just leave it to me
So now u know how my name came to be

What am I going to do next?
Y'all just wait and see
Just remember I'm the key!
I'm a smooth talka
Open up the locka
Who am I? I'm Soulshocka!!

Hook

it's shocking, how I rhyme this way
it's shocking, who I was and who i am today
it's shocking, I might mock ya
who am I? I'm Soulshocka

it's shocking, how I rhyme this way
it's shocking, who I was and who I am today
it's shocking, poppin up like Orville Redenbocka
who am I? I'm Soulshocka

Who Am I?

Original rap by R. Wyles from the title "Who am I?"

Produced by Josh Lucas

Rap produced by Sam Kingston

Who am I? That's a rhetorical question
When you start confessing better check your blessing
No second guessing.
Who am I? There's a lot about me
How can you doubt me?
Taking shots at me
I can be mesmerizing
When you start apologizing
What you're doing is plagiarizing
It can be far more exciting
But you're out there fighting
With the dust that you're biting
It's a philosophy
A reverse psychology
Is there anything that you can offer me?
We're the chosen few
Not much, but what can you do
And if you all be hearing me
I am the frequency of creativity
Love's a thing you can't destroy
Love's a thing you can't avoid
Love's the strongest force of all

So come and love you one and all
I'm gonna dare to it,
share to it,
declare to it
You gotta love it.

Dancing on the Ceiling

Lyrics by Rio Wyles
Produced by Joe Seabe for PASW

Chorus

Take me baby, dancing on the ceiling
Make me feel like I'm number one.
Hold up, Shorty (Chorus repeats)
Comin to the spot
Make it extra hot
see whatcha got
Gimme me an adrenalin rush
Seeing you blush
feeling your touch
Oooww so much
Maybe it's a crush
See, it's off the meter
You're hot like a heater
I needed some lovin'
You're warm like an oven
Just like a stove
Let's get it cooking
Mommy used to say
"Hey, good looking."
This vibration's got us shookin'
Get on the floor
That's not the dealing'
Oh for realin'
My way of chillin'
Let's go dancing on the ceiling

Hook

Going up

Going up

Turning you around

Around

Up to the top

Top

Show me whatcha got

Got

Trippin' from above, Shorty

We will fall in love

It's a crazy feeling

So appealing

When we're dancing on the ceiling

Chorus

Take me baby, dancing on the ceiling

So here we go

Make me feel like I'm number one.

Take me baby, dancing on the ceiling

Let's hit the flo'

Make me feel like I'm number one.

Upside down

Back to the front

It's realistic

Not a stunt.

Comin' up behind

It's a surprise

Let's recognize

It's not a crime
It's just a sign
Cherry wine
Girl you're the sweetest I could find
Up in the air without a care
I stop (full stop)
and stare.
Girl you look fine
When we grind and wind
Floating in time
It's contagious
All these movements
Are outrageous
So flirtatious
Goodness gracious
Like a storybook turn the pages
I haven't done this ish for ages
Going thru mazes
It's quite a feeling
When we're dancing on the ceiling

Hook

Going up
Going up
Turning you around
Around
Up to the top
Top
Show me whatcha got
Got

Trippin' from above, Shorty
We will fall in love
It's a crazy feeling
So appealing
When we're dancing on the ceiling

Chorus
Take me baby, dancing on the ceiling
So here we go
Make me feel like I'm number one.
Take me baby, dancing on the ceiling
Let's hit the flo'
Make me feel like I'm number one.
It's a gravitational evolution
A vertical reconstitution
So get your rise on
In the fly zone
Party of the year
So get on up
over here
and glide with me round a chandelier
It's blazing fire
so amazing
so let's go higher
and dance among the stars
Let's hit the bars
on the moon, Neptune or maybe Mars.
There's not a limit
when you're in it
Believe me Shorty it's not a gimmick

There's not a feeling
so appealing
as when you're dancing on the ceiling

Hook
Going up
Going up
Turning you around
Around
Up to the top
Top
Show me whacha got
Got
Trippin' from above, Shorty
We will fall in love
It's a crazy feeling
So appealing
When we're dancing on the ceiling

Chorus
Take me baby, dancing on the ceiling
So here we go
Make me feel like I'm number one.
Take me baby, dancing on the ceiling
Let's hit the flo'
Make me feel like I'm number one.
Yah, that's what I'm talkin' about
Make me feel like I'm number one.
Leaving foot prints on the ceiling, y'all

Make me feel like I'm number one.
Soulshaka for you.
Make me feel like I'm number one.
I'm out.
Make me feel like I'm number one.

Stand Up To Cancer
Award-winning rap by Rio Wyles
Produced by Sam Kingston

This is for all the people
Came a long way
Still have a long way to go
What're you gotta do?
Just stand up.
Yall. Yall.
Is this what life is all about?
Got you feeling like no one cares
When you're stuck so far from your destination
Gotta wonder why it's so unfair
I know it seems like this load is so hard to bear
But hold on you'll get where you need to go
Just hold out your hand
Yeah, we'll meet you there
Right between recovery and having hope
You gotta love now till there's no tomorrow
Like to give a shout out to my homie Carl
Rest in peace said to say he ain't here today
Dark clouds in the sky
I'm a clear the way
Just hear me say, Uh
People live your life
Yeah, we'll never fall down
Yeah we'll stand and fight

Just stay in the light
Cause it's not your time
And you still got a whole lot of mountains to climb
So, stand up!

Clear to See
Lyrics by Rio Wyles
Produced by Joe Seabe

I've been hangin on
It's been way too long
All this time you've been on my mind
Watchin you on this road
I've been longing for the time
When you are mine
Maybe that's a sign
That I'm about to incline
Longing
For it to carry on
You feel you've been holding on
Let it go, pass it on,
Crime is a sign
Let it entwine
Watch the magic happen
Taking control
Taking hold
Of this psychedelic mold

Chorus
If it's meant to be
You'll be here with me
If we can agree
This relationship's charging a fee

Follow me
You're sweet as tea
On the count of three it's clear to see
We've been on this road before, so I've been told
Waiting for this moment to unfold
You come from out of the blue so true
What we've been through
How much we knew
Time passed while we grew
Oh, my dear
We're outta' here
Let's not let this moment disappear
Looking at your reflection in the mirror
Like a satellite
On the edge burning bright
Like a light bulb
About to explode
So many problems that we can solve
But it's hard to get involved
With this tension
The hesitation in moving in the right direction
We just have to clear it to make it perfection.

Chorus

If it's meant to be
You'll be here with me
If we can agree
This relationship's charging a fee
Follow me
You're sweet as tea
On the count of three it's clear to see

Did I forget to mention?
You're a lot to handle
So many things that I could say
But hey you brighten up my day
You're very appealing
And a maximizing healing
The feeling's like an earthquake
So much that I can take
I think I'm ready
You're beautiful
Like a painting from the Getty
We can make it thru
So quick not long overdue
In its state
In its hands
This is where it stands
We've gotten off the brink I think
And somehow we're still in sync
Working it out
Without a doubt
We're strong
Don't let this moment pass on

Chorus

If it's meant to be
You'll be here with me
If we can agree
This relationship's charging a fee
Follow me
You're sweet as tea

On the count of three it's clear to see

We Will Prevail

Lyrics by Rio Wyles
Produced by Joe Seabe for PASW

Intro

Feels like we're stranded
Yo!
Plane hasn't landed.
Soulshocka for you
Folks out here abandoned.
All the people in the occupy movement I gotch ya. Keep your head up.
Somehow I know we will prevail.
NYC. KILLADELPHIA. OAKTOWN. PTOWN. SEATOWN.
Droppin' with no bottom
Problems we ain't solvin
Yo the recession
What's your confession?
The isolation and the obligation
Globalization really smashed and hit the nation.
In heavy rotation.
Like a Dominos fallin.
It's a calling.
Getting back to normal
Is out of the equation
It don't seem real
More like animation.
The expectating
The waiting is frustrating.
Why won't it fade off?

All the workers laid off
Politicians paid off.
Madoff.
Thru the trials and tribulations
While the banks go south on vacation.

Pre-Hook

Walkin in a straight line and never look back
Never surrender when you're under attack
Won't be easy but you gotta stay strong
Never give up cause the road is long.

Hook

Feels like we're stranded
Feels like we're stranded
Plane hasn't landed.
Plane hasn't landed.
Folks out here abandoned.
It ain't the way
It's ain't the way they planned it.
Feels like we're stranded
Feels like we're stranded
Plane hasn't landed.
Plane hasn't landed.
Folks out here abandoned.
C'mon
Somehow I know we will prevail.

Verse 2

Refuse the abuse before it's let loose.

Wanting to call a truce.
On the employment line
You're annoyed this time
Finally at the counter all you get is a fine.
Nothin but swine stealing dimes
wasting other people's time
And you tryin to survive with the other 99
And you're mcdivin
They're high fivin
What's with the creation of this frustration?
A re-evaluation
Turn the radio change the station
It's a game of Truth or Dare
The rich don't seem to care
What seems unfair is fair
Prepare
There's a mission that you're dissin
And if you're talkin you can't listen
Shhhhh!

Pre-Hook

Walkin in a straight line and never look back
Never surrender when you're under attack
Won't be easy but you gotta stay strong
Never give up cause the road is long.

Hook

Feels like we're stranded
Feels like we're stranded

Plane hasn't landed.
Plane hasn't landed
Folks out here abandoned.
It ain't the way
It ain't the way they planned it.
Feels like we're stranded
Feels like we're stranded
Plane hasn't landed.
Plane hasn't landed.
Folks out here abandoned.
C'mon
Somehow I know we will prevail.

Verse 2

It's like a battle of Mortal Combat
Try to get beyond that
Another hack keeps us getting on track
People say we're the future
But the future looks blurry.
Déjà vu like Bill Murray
Rats on a ship scurry with no worry.
Hurry.
Take a car to Guttenberg
Union City
Or Queens.
By any means.
You don't know what's going on behind the scenes
You might get lucky and I'll spill the beans
So many traitors and so many fiends
We're being worn out like a pile of jeans

Holy cow
We might throw in the towel
Like a finale
And it's time to take a bow
What are we going to do now?
Liberate
For goodness sake
Why would you wait when the world's at stake.

Pre-Hook

Walkin in a straight line and never look back
Never surrender when you're under attack
Won't be easy but you gotta stay strong
Never give up cause the road is long.

Hook

Feels like we're stranded.
Everyone out there struggling
Feels like we're stranded.
Grinding. Working the 9 to 5
For almost nothing at all
Feels like we're stranded.
Carrying all the weight.
Folks out here abandoned.
The oppressed pushed down.
Knocked to the sidelines
To my dogs in the Dave (U.C. Davis)
Feels like we're stranded
Beantown. Madtown. L.A.

Folks out here abandoned.
Santiago. Barcelona. Damascus. Roma.
Somehow I know we will prevail.
We will not fail. We will prevail.
Somehow I know we will prevail.
We will not fail. We will prevail.
Somehow I know we will prevail.
Yeah.
Dream big, y'all.
Soulshocka
I'm out.

Yonkers Remix
Lyrics by Rio Wyles
Track by Tyler the Creator

Runnin in circles in the middle of the hall
Searching and rushing like the middle of the mini mall
Examining these politicians
Read the descriptions
Occupy mission
While my people have no tuition
If I pushed the play button am I going into submission?
Hell naw, cuz I'm a keep the tradition
I see malice in these palaces
Take the dialysis, people suffocating
While they sippin from their chalices
Royal like Excalibur
Your music is like brocolli
Homie I ain't havin it
had a bit, but it
Wack as ish

Hook

Yeah this Yonkers
Damn this ish is bonkers
The man about to conquer
My mama made a Monster
Yeah this Yonkers
Damn this ish is bonkers

The man about to conquer
Stompin these imposters
I sign inscriptions, write this Pulp Fiction,
Dudes think they can spit, shoulda waited for the Voice audition
Sitting back in my zone, hear a knock at the door
blabbering on the phone, I ain't kickin back no more
Low and behold, my flow didn't drop below
These fools like oh dang, sh**, Holy mackerel
Watch me heat it up like some Tuna casserole
About to have a moment,
So now you have to go

Hook

Yeah this Yonkers
Damn this ish is bonkers
The man about to conquer
My mama made a Monster
Yeah this Yonkers
Damn this ish is bonkers
The man about to conquer
Stompin these imposters
Remove the leeches, increases the grow zone
Call me E.T., I microphone home
And I defy gravity like the flight academy
And It's a travesty how these fools Back-stabbing me
Doctor said I had a flu, what should I do?
Should I go and screw, mind my ones and twos? Chill a month or two?
Guess it's up to you,

Cuz my apron's stainless
Pardon all my language,
I'm on my English
Take the repercussion, most ain't hittin nothing,
Start up with that Bluffin, huh, end of discussion.
Yeah this Yonkers
Damn this ish is bonkers
The man about to conquer
My mama made a Monster
Yeah this Yonkers
Damn this ish is bonkers
The man about to conquer
Stompin these,
stompin these imposters

No Lie Remix

Lyrics by Rio Wyles
Track by Mike WiLL Made It

Verse 1

I've been thinking about the past, how to make it last
Too much fishy stuff, I'm just takin out the trash
Keep moving like George Jefferson, Trynna get on like a settlement
And I'ma make you sound like you got a speech impediment
You just keep on meddling, I'ma keep on peddling
Movin down this road, till I find a place I can settle in
From where the nights are dim, Parts of my town are kinda grim
Sucka MCs getting drowned out, get to the surface you gotta swim
And this is my mission, flowins my ambition
I'm keep on being hungry and there is no nutrition
I take the mold out
when I roll out
Change the degrees, hot or cold out
Just getting started, haven't sold out
Flatten the game watch it fold out

Pre- Chorus
Makin the game transition

I'ma keep on going, there ain't no intermission
No lie, no lie, no lie-e-i-e-i
No lie, no lie, no lie-e-i-e-i

Chorus

All my people say true, I ain't never told no lie, I ain't never told no lie
All my people say true, I ain't never told no lie, I ain't never told no lie
All my people say true, I ain't never told no lie, I ain't never told no lie
That's a thing I don't do, nah I just do it for my people who be trynna
make a mill before they die, hold-up

Verse 2

Solo like Chewbacca, me I came to mock ya
Came to play to the game, we can shoot it out like Soccer
You're sugar coated like Willy Wonka,
Yeah I don't need no pessimists
Let's start addressin this,
you don't wanna mess with this
Heating it up, rip em to shreds, making it hard to come back,
Why you bout that lurkin mayn, I'm pushin em down like a thumbtack
Commotion's going down, short circuit, The fuse is blowing
Gonna get it straight, yeah I gotta get the juices flowing,
Too much fashion, too much taxin, Why you asking? This my passion
Too many Comedians like Monty python
Got to get it right, yep that's a tight one

Tricky like Dennis the menace, Play the game like tennis
Going through these leaps and bounds, you can see my flow's tremendous

Verse 3

Grabbin the beat
Stabbin the beat
Telling these fools Go back to sleep
We can have a meet n greet, in the street,
Dog in the heat, causin defeat
Goin through Trials and tribulations'
It's hard to change the situation
Hitting em up no hesitation
Participation for the Invasion
Like I said, just turn the station
double art, counter creation
Pentagon, I stand beyond
Wrap it up and pass the baton,
Jumping thru these Obstacles
Eatin' em up like popsicles
Following trends is optional
But being a leader is logical
Getting very hypnotic, yeah I think I got it,
Keep pushing forward, gotta hit the hydraulics
Lotta rappers sounding robotic
Like a fan I circulate
Never mumble I articulate
Cause commotion I regulate
Gotta go hard For goodness sake
"The Aftermath" (in progress)

It's like the weather
You'll be droppin like the rain
Goin down the drain
Cryin out in pain.
It's a bloody shame
No one else to blame.
All of it in vain.
Cause you're out of the commission
You all better listen.
While you're turning the ignition.
You're about to audition
Not for the boss, but the mortician.

Chorus

It's empty out there
In the middle of nowhere
Get out if you dare.
Without a care.
Beware.
Cause you're trapped on a path
Feel the rise of the wrath
Leading to the aftermath
"Over Again"
You know, life has its days
So do people.
And Life has its possibilities.
And so do people.
One day I was walkin out.
Tryin to clear my mind
Know what I'm talking about.

There's nothing in life but an explanation
All you really need is some meditation.
Not medication just demonstration.
Cause it's for my manner. You're madder
then a mad hatter.
Commercial, you've got a rehearsal
History is not admitted, but in the pressure you just can't
quit it.
You gotta run out. Don't worry about it. Just walk it out.
Just walk it off.
Just picture me rolling, strolling in an atmosphere.
This can't be here. This can't be happening here.
See it's blazing hot. Standing right on the spot.
You know strange things happening all around you.
Just like karma's come around and it found you.
It's happening again.
She's right behind you.
You know, it's happening again.
Deep inside you.
You know I've been here before.
I'm trapped in time.
it's happening again.
Tryin to make you mine.
You know it's happening again. Ahhh. All over again. Ahhh.
All over again, Ahhh. All over and over again.
You know in life things happen.
doesn't seem what it seems.
Even in dreams.
obstacles may appear.
you may not know when you're here.

and time and place and when
it may happen over again.
one day u figure it out.
what your life was all about.
look at the messages comin after you
and what you're about to do.
explain it straight to the core.
This is what life is for.
protozoaic time of waste
shining in the United States
don't worry it won't be too late
be here at the right time and place.
It's happening again.
she's right behind you.
You know, it's happening again.
deep inside you.
you know I've been here before.
trapped in time.
it's happening again.
tryin to make you mine.
it's happening again. Ahhh.
all over again. Ahhh.
all over again. Ahhh.
all over and over again.
all over again.
Explanation is the key of life.
you know you'll make it alright.
tonight girl you're mine
why is it so hard to find?
are you blind?

We gotta make this relationship flow
I need to know?
why are you haunting me?
quit taunting me
it's like déjà vu.
do you feel it too?
this everlasting pride
that I hold deep inside.
now tell me how you feel.
see if our love is real.
let's take this to another level.
and let it settle.
now come into my time machine
you beauty queen
not just another sweet sixteen
cause you know in the end
it will happen over again.
It's happening again.
she's right behind you.
You know, it's happening again.
deep inside you.
you know i've been here before.
trapped in time.
it's happening again.
tryin to make you mine.
it's happening again. ahhh.
all over again. ahhh.
all over and over again.
all over again.

Collision Course
Lyrics by Rio Wyles
Produced by Joe Seabe

INTRO
Everyone has a struggle
Some find their way out of it
But others, end up in a danger zone
Called a collision course.

Verse 1
Look see you are not me
Times up at the count of three
The frequency of the Trilogy
Saying you don't know me
Keeping score of this tug of war
Is a bore
Evolve
A puzzle that you can't solve
Life's an alibi
That you reptify
That you can't deny
Well, I heard it all before, yeah
Mr High on the Coast
Anything that you want the most
Thinking you're the Host
Watch it all disappear like a ghost
Next step to a con man

Why you mother-fuckin' fond of them?
Your days are numbered and you're on ten
And you may not get to do this again

Hook

Packing my bags and I'm on my way
Times up and it ends today
Going down you don't want to help
It's killing me that you're killing yourself
Packing my bags and I'm on my way
Times up and it ends today
Going down you don't want to help
It's killing me that you're killing yourself

Verse 2

Overdosin' have a ball
Folks like zombies heading to the mall
Pretty young things you want to hit 'em all
Line 'em up and watch 'em fall
So now it's come to this
I've had enough of your eager bliss
Cause here's the twist
It finishes where it started off
With you're being pissed
And the only way out
Is through a desert of drought
It's like a heavy weight bout
I think you know what I'm talking about
Beyond the edge of the walk of life

Where you're ling is a mountain of strife
Ah shit no remorse
Is leading you down a collision course

Hook

Packing my bags and I'm on my way
Times up and it ends today
Going down you don't want to help
It's killing me that you're killing yourself
Packing my bags and I'm on my way
Times up and it ends today
Going down you don't want to help
It's killing me that you're killing yourself

Verse 3

A renegade about to be saved
Dead of winter in a heat wave
One step from a close shave
Dancing with the devil on your own grave
I'm not blaming you
The struggle you've been through
But now it's up to you
Sucke what you gonna do?
Well, you think it'sa game
Well, you think it's a shame
Suddenly the cameras are flashing
No more harrassing
Time is passing
Minutes are ticking

Adrenalin's kicking
So many regrets you gotta be thinking
Cause it's quicksand and you're sinking
But it ain't too late to turn back
Packing my bags and I'm on my way
Times up and it ends today
Going down you don't want to help
It's killing me that you're killing yourself
Packing my bags and I'm on my way
Times up and it ends today
Going down you don't want to help
It's killing me that you're killing yourself
Packing my bags and I'm on my way
C'mon
On my way
C'mon
On my way
You don't have to be forced
But that road you're on is nothing but a collision course
Get ready
I'm coming

Choose Love

Shakti Ma Ft
Lyrics by Rio Wyles - Soulshocka
Produced by Bob de Marco

Hani Ananna
Hold on a little longa
Find your way to higher ground
Don't know if you're lost or found
Imagine a world in harmony
But if that's to be
According to plan
Take it to the common man
Try not to fear one another
Son of a gun cause he might be your brother
Have an aspiration
O with levitation
Through the condemnation
To be equipped to co-exist in bliss
Know what it's all for
In this game of tug of war
Open the door
Settle the score
Reach for solidarity
Get some clarity
It's a rarity
Do I dare go this conscious?
I would if I could
Do you think I should?

Appendix II
A Few Short Writings

Unemployment as Divine Appointment

"I don't want any plastics! And I don't want any ground floors!"
George Bailey, "It's a Wonderful Life"
"Hush... somebody's calling your name."

Author unknown

I was a person who based my security on the things of this world. I was in success mode: First rate education followed by good jobs, upward mobility, and advancement. I was set. Then, I began to take chances, abandoning two lucrative careers to pursue dreams. And it paid off. But, interestingly, the real journey, the real riches only began during a period of unemployment, an event that in the past would have set off all kinds of alarms and panic buttons. But not this time.

This time it led to an awakening. And in a moment my life was transformed as the veil was lifted, and unemployment took on a new meaning. It transformed from panic to opportunity. Where I once saw lack, I now experienced as opportunity. Time off for reading and meditation, revelation and discovery of God. Time to just hang out in that vibration. To fully leave the things of this world, and begin to know another. I still don't know where the money came from during that period, but it did. And when the time was right to make certain moves, important moves that required money, a job serendipitously appeared that allowed me to grow further and expand. And to realize that God, not Paramount, is my sufficiency in all things. Or that Paramount was simply the vehicle of my abundance.

And that unemployment was nothing less than an appointment with the Divine. That led to a life filled with joy, not dependent on success or circumstances. And one that is truly rich.

So to all of you out there reading this who find yourself unemployed or fearing you're about to be, in this moment of high global transformation, don't despair. In fact, rejoice.

It's God calling. Just for you. And it's an appointment you definitely want to keep.

Seek the Kingdom first, and all else shall indeed be added.

Dream Big

Let the river run,
Let all the dreamers
Wake the nation.
Come, the New Jerusalem.
Carly Simon, "Let the River Run"
But when he was still a great way off, his father saw him...
ran....and kissed him.

Luke 15:20

What if the greatest dream we could have was to know God?

Every Friday when my son was growing up, we'd head to Tower for a CD to celebrate his week. Tower was a place where he was completely at home, where he felt like he belonged, where hardly anyone stared. One such Friday while perusing the bins, he piped up: "I want to be in the music business." For me, it was a fleeting moment into Rio, without autism.

It had been a tough week, full of testing. The Doctor sat me down and told me to get real. That my expectations for Rio's ability to grow were unfair to him. So, I 'got real' and asked, 'Do you want to work here?' Rio looked at me. 'I want to be a rapper and own my own label. You got to dream bigger than that, Mom.'

A rapper? Impossible. His language was usually nonsensical and endlessly repetitive.

Then, I was awakened, filled with joy and my whole life changed. I'd met God. And left my Hollywood dream behind and began a walk in the miraculous, as I meditated with my son and the autism began to disappear and language appeared.

I was reminded of all this recently when an old friend dropped in. A movie idea. For Batman. Batman's a closed franchise, off limits. No way. But after a spectacular trial run of the pitch, the music showed up on the p.a. as I shopped in Ralph's. A sign? For me? The answer came immediately on a t-shirt cruising by. 'Dream Big.'

And as I write this we're headed to New York where Rio will be rapping at Carnegie Hall.

Will Batman sell? It doesn't matter, cause I see an ever bigger dream on this road I'm on. Just ahead.

God

Wall Street, Main Street and God Street

"Television should come with a warning – dangerous to ones' health."

Rev. Michael Bernard Beckwith

I've had trouble lately, keeping my mind on Truth. I mean, can you blame me? This story that's unfolding is one humdinger. And to make matters worse, I'm hooked on the myth.

It's a story that's miraculous, but right now it's one that makes me sad, choose sides, feel like crying, or anxious, out of nowhere. And sometimes very angry.

I'm hooked. It's gotta stop.

I take it into meditation. Revelation: This is God's story. Let it unfold.

Worst case -- it will be an amazing opportunity to love.

So true. But I'm still hooked. Still watching MSNBC.

Then I read Emmet Fox's discourse on Noah. I, like Noah, had built an ark, over these last years, through prayer and meditation. But, the specs that Noah divinely received, I learned, had no portholes, no window, but one. At the very top. Looking up. Only up. So, when the flood began, there was no checking out the flood waters every two hours. Not for Noah. But I could. I snuck in a porthole and kept looking out in wonder and amazement that the story was really happening. And anger at certain players. I was in the thick of duality. And my sadness returned.

Then, I took it silently into a prayer circle And, as I sat in that high vibration, I saw all the players on the world scene I wanted to rail against, in a curtain call, with me, hands raised, all smiling, taking a bow. I smiled and chuckled at the image. And regained my perspective. That we're all in this together, this journey of our soul, individually and collectively. That we are all one. God. And I stepped out, back to where I belong.

Rapunzel, Let Down Your Hair

"Master, where are you dwelling?
Come and see....Follow me"
John 1:39; John 1:43

Recently I was approached by a woman, who'd heard about the work I'm doing with my son, struck hard by autism. For a few years I've been praying and meditating with him every day, and the healing is nothing short of miraculous. The woman had a compelling interest. Two of her grandchildren are diagnosed, and the older, a girl, is almost completely non-verbal and increasingly violent.

That first day as we meditated, I treated for peace, harmony, and words to flow effortlessly. On the second, the woman began to tell me their story, of a mother who'd become a witch and the younger boy who throws rolls of paper off a balcony muttering "Rapunzel." I gasped. Could this story be operating in their lives? In ours?

Rapunzel is not your typical guy saves girl kinda' story. It starts out that way, but the plan is discovered, the Prince blinded, and the Girl, well she loses her hair and is tossed out into the Wilderness. There she is forced to grow out of victimhood into her genuine power. And in the end, it's her song that leads the blind prince out of the dark forest, and the salt water of her tears that restore his sight.

A big part of this journey for me has been that wilderness experience, lonely at first, but full of riches. That day as we sat in *my* wilderness, I saw this girl bust out of her dungeon, take dominion and SPEAK! And that night when the grandmother called home, her son excitedly reported in that his daughter had begun to do just that. Speak. And is it just coincidence that the same day a young woman in Austria, held captive for years, fled her dungeon, not fully understanding what made her run at that moment?

From the wilderness...

Appendix III
Recommended Reading

Marianne Williamson *A Return to Love*

Gary Zukov *Seat of the Soul*

Gloria Karpinski *Where Two World's Touch, Barefoot on Holy Ground*

Thomas Moore *The Re-enchantment of Everyday Life*

Neal Donald Walsh *Conversations with God* (CD preferred)

Iyanla Vanzant *One Day My Soul Just Opened Up* (CD preferred)

Christian Larsen *A Pathway of Roses*

Joel Goldsmith *The Journey Back to My Father's House, The Art of Spiritual Healing*
Once you're into Goldsmith, they're all worth reading.

Tai Malachi *The Gospel of Thomas*

John A. Sanford *The Tragedy of King Saul, The Gospel of John, The Journey Within, Keys to the Kingdom, Dreams: God's Forgotten Language*

Fritz Kunkel *Creation Continues*

Carl Jung *Memories, Dreams, Reflections*

Edward F. Edinger *The Archetype of the Apocalypse, The Christian Archetype*

Howard Thurman *Meditations of the Heart*

Carolyn Myss *Sacred Contracts*

Michael Beckwith *Forty Day Mind Fast and Soul Feast, Inner Space Odyssey, CD set*

Joseph Campbell *The Power of Myth*, DVD

Margaret Starbird *The Woman With the Alabaster Jar*

Emmet Fox *The Sermon on the Mount*

Guru Mayi *The Yoga of Discipline*

And I save the best for last,

Hopefully, with new eyes and understanding,

The Bible

Made in the USA
San Bernardino, CA
28 April 2018